# generation
# DEBT

## Take Control of Your Money
### *A How-to Guide*

## CARMEN WONG ULRICH

WARNER
BUSINESS
BOOKS™

NEW YORK    BOSTON

This publication is designed to provide competent and reliable information regarding the subject matter covered. However, it is sold with the understanding that the author and publisher are not engaged in rendering legal, financial, or other professional advice. Laws and practices often vary from state to state and if legal or other expert assistance is required, the services of a professional should be sought. The author and publisher specifically disclaim any liability that is incurred from the use or application of the contents of this book.

*Book design and text composition by Stratford Publishing Services*

*Cover design by Erin Sharpe*

Warner Business Books
Warner Books

Time Warner Book Group
1271 Avenue of the Americas, New York, NY 10020
Visit our Web site at www.twbookmark.com.

The Warner Business Books logo is a trademark of Warner Books.

Printed in the United States of America

First Edition: January 2006

10  9  8  7  6  5  4  3  2  1

Library of Congress Cataloging-in-Publication Data

Ulrich, Carmen Wong.
Generation debt : take control of your money : a how-to guide / Carmen Wong Ulrich.
     p.  cm.
Includes index.
ISBN 0-446-69543-2
1. Young adults—Finance, Personal.   2. Finance, Personal.   3. Debt.   I. Title.
HG179.U42   2006
332.024′02′0842—dc22                                                    2005022148

*For the "G" Girls,*
**Nina, Mickey, Josie & Lola**

# ACKNOWLEDGMENTS

The support and encouragement of a great bunch of people was instrumental in making this book happen. First of all, *un million gracias* to my beloved Lawrence. His love, support, and refreshingly candid advice were gifts more valuable than he knows. Miles of gratitude to my former boss, dear mentor, and friend Sheryl Tucker. I am also deeply and forever thankful to another former boss, mentor, and great friend, Bob Safian. B, you got me started. I was lucky enough to also have a badass cheerleader, my longtime, dear friend Isabel Gonzalez. One more lady had a direct impact on this book, my smarty-pants youngest sister, research assistant, fact checker, and photographer, Laura "Lola" Giannotti. Thank you so much for working on this with me. And to my dad, Charlie Giannotti, who had seven-year-old me run into the local store for his *Wall Street Journal* every morning, thanks for instilling in me some great money habits. I didn't think it was cool then, but it's pretty cool now. Thanks, Pop.

I will also always be grateful for the professional support, guidance, encouragement, and availability of some wonderfully fine folks who've lent me their ears, time, and wisdom over the past couple of years: John Huey, Angelo Figueroa, Susan Casey, Roy Johnson, Carolina Buia, Maria Baugh, Jeannie Park, Jean Chatzky, Peter Castro, Denise Martin, Suzanne Woolley, Michelle

Ebanks, Datwon Thomas, Lang Whitaker, Andy Borinstein, and Doug King.

Another bucket of gratitude goes to my wonderful agent who breaks the mold and whom I am so glad to have had the serendipity of working with, Claudia Cross. And finally, many writers would be so lucky to have such an editor as Dan Ambrosio. What a pleasure working with you on this, Dan. Thanks so much for taking me on.

# CONTENTS

## CHAPTER 3
### Master Your Student Loans

## CHAPTER 4
### The Potential Prison of Credit Card Debt

## CHAPTER 5
### To Rent, Perchance to Buy

## CHAPTER 6
### The Need for Wheels

## CHAPTER 7
### Honor the Tax Man

## CHAPTER 8
### The Golden Net of Insurance

## CHAPTER 9
### The Magical 401 (k)

## CHAPTER 10
### A Pricey Future

# INTRODUCTION

*Shhhhhh* . . . You hear that? That's the sound of millions of eighteen- to thirty-four-year-olds getting sucked in, pulled down, and held under by debt.

But wait, aren't these flush times? The market is up, job creation and hiring rates are getting back on track, interest rates and inflation remain low, spending continues to rise, and home-ownership is at record levels.

Damn those dastardly baby boomers and their dividend tax cuts, outsourcing drama, looming retirement, and cheating CEOs. They've stolen the country's economic spotlight for too long. It's time to turn some serious attention to young adults—the next generation of big consumers, earners, taxpayers, home-owners, parents, and CEOs. Because America, we're in trouble.

It behooves me to call this book *Generation Debt*. But the sad, sick truth is that young adults today are drowning in debt—so if the phrase fits (and helps), let's wear it. And contrary to what many (older) folks believe, this debt is not mostly credit card debt. According to Student Monitor, a leading market research firm, a 2002 survey found that of the average $18,560 graduating college students expect to owe when they leave school, 99 percent is student loan debt.

From there, the picture only gets worse. To add to that giant

"ANGRY
YOUNG
&
POOR"

—printed on a sweatshirt
by Newbreed Girl in
Alloy catalog, 2004

five-figure debt load that starts draw-ing blood six months after graduation, a newly minted college grad needs sharp clothes to interview in, an up-to-date computer and cell phone, and a car to drive to work or monthly pass to com-mute on public transport. If the option of living at home is not there, there's first and last month's rent to pay, furni-ture to sleep and sit on, clothes to wash, insurance to buy, and food to eat. And lest we forget, many young adults need to pay for their own health insurance.

All this, starting at around $28,000 a year.

We are the most debt-burdened generation ever produced (I'm talking about the young adult generation of eighteen to thirty-four-year-olds). We are also the most highly educated, technologically advanced, ethnically and racially diverse, cre-ative group of adults on the planet. Our contributions in tech-nology, culture, entrepreneurship, social services, and media are already immense and revolutionary.

Yet we are fined for our ambition. Up straight, we are "fined" for the costs demanded of us in order to get ahead. It's a quasi-tax levied on us for wanting a college education, a good career, getting paid well for something we enjoy doing, the security of health care, a piece of the fat and tasty American pie.

It has become too easy for young adults in this country to get trapped by the cycle of ambition. The state of the American job market now requires a minimum of a college degree to get an interview for an upward-track post that pays us barely enough to get by—not to mention paying the loans we had to get for the degree to get the job in the first place. And when it comes to advanced degrees, we've all heard about the state of doctors, graduating with an MD and already six figures in debt. At least they can typically look forward to a high starting salary. Imagine the new PhD who ends up more than $100,000 in debt and whose next rung on the career ladder is a fellowship research position at $30,000 a year. Absurd.

We need cell phones and the latest computers. We have to look good and present ourselves as the brand of "me." We have to compete in the workforce with Joe and Jane, whose parents probably paid for their college education and living expenses in full and now pay for their rent and credit cards, too.

Does anyone else see a disparity here?

What about retirement? Ask a room of eighteen- to thirty-four-year-olds about retirement and you'll hear everything from "Huh?" to "Re-*what*-ment?" to "Man, I'm just trying to pay my rent." In the fairly recent past, as soon as a young adult landed a solid full-time job it was the norm to start saving for retirement, because heck, it was only twenty to thirty years away. Now we'll probably live past eighty-five, the thought of a stereotypical retirement is akin to a slow death, and, as the U.S. Government Accountability Office recently reported, without reform Social Security funds will be gone by 2042. We're a different bunch. Working nine-to-five, a lifelong career at a public company with a pension, a single job track for life: These things don't ring very true for us today.

So where's our payoff? Why are we penalized so expensively for wanting to get a college education or even a graduate education? Why are our bank accounts punished if we need and want internships in creative or academic fields that pay almost nothing, forcing us to live off our credit cards, pay for our own health care costs, and work second and third jobs just to get ahead? Unlike the generations before us who had much lower education costs and nearly twice the amount of help from the government (Pell Grants, at their inception in the early 1970s, financed up to 84 percent of college tuition, whereas the max Pell Grant now contributes closer to 40 percent), why are we subject to an "ambition tax"? Why are we paying such a big, painful price for wanting to get ahead? And what can we do about it?

# generation
# DEBT

# Why Do We Have
# So Much Debt, Anyway?

### *The Costs of Trying to Make It*

In order to master your enemy, it's best to get familiar with its MO.

So before helping you tackle, manage, and come out on top of the eight-hundred-pound gorilla of your personal money situation, let me offer you a quick tour of the confluence of events that have gotten many of us stuck in this tight financial spot in the first place.

Worst-case scenario, the following section will make you look supersavvy at your next cocktail party. Best-case scenario, it will piss you off, make you wise, and get you moving.

## WHY AND HOW A COLLEGE EDUCATION
## HAS BECOME A MUST

Notice how there is less and less mention these days of "upper class" or "lower class"? How marketers and advertisers (and

**$554**
**$964**

average earnings per week of a
high school graduate vs. a
college graduate

**16.1%**
6.4%

unemployment rate for average
high school graduate vs. college
graduate

—U.S. Dept. of Labor, 2003

politicians) now segment Americans with phrases such as *hippie boomers, soccer moms, NASCAR dads, tweeners, bobos,* and *urban singles?*

**Lifestyle** has replaced the old-fashioned concept of social class. The very positive power of lifestyle as the standard of social segmentation is that lifestyles can be built by choice, not by birth. And the rest of the world is rapidly following suit. (Hooray for that!)

But here's the kicker: For most Americans, education is the key to lifestyle. And as we all know only too painfully well, education costs.

The shiny side of this penny—and what we can pretty much deduce on our own—was confirmed recently by the U.S. Department of Labor in its report *Working in the 21st Century:* College graduates age twenty-five and over **earn nearly twice as much** as workers who stopped their education with a high school diploma.

Many folks got that notice. The Census Bureau reported in June 2004 that Americans are more educated than ever before, with 85 percent of all adults twenty-five and older completing

* This is a particular favorite of mine—short for "bourgeois bohemians." Check out *Bobos in Paradise: The New Upper Class and How They Got There,* by David Brooks, for the scoop on this powerful bunch.

high school that year and 27 percent having a bachelor's degree in 2003—a historic high.

For comparison, in 1975, 18 percent of men and 11 percent of women had a college degree. In 2000, those numbers rose to 28 percent of men and

> **28%**
> **60%**
> _____
> percent of jobs requiring at least some college—1970s vs. now
> —U.S. Dept. of Labor, 2003

24 percent of women. Nice catch-up job, ladies and gentlemen.

Then again, I still (unfortunately) hear ranting justifications like "College is nothing more than a piece of paper." Or another favorite, "I'll learn on my own and start my own business—Bill Gates didn't finish college!" Well, I see men wearing leather sandals, too, but that don't make them Jesus. I digress.

Straight entrepreneurship is a challenging, potentially lucrative, but extremely risky way to go. If you can do it without getting a college degree, more power to you, all the luck in the world. However, if you are planning on joining the workforce and getting a good j-o-b, that "piece of paper" is your key. Why? Because as those of you who have completed college, are in college, or have had any college know, to succeed in undergraduate and especially graduate school, it takes discipline, motivation, dedication, book learnin', and a major dose of experimentation and growing up, not to mention a big chunk out of your and your parents' wallet. So an employer is much more likely to take you (college-educated person) seriously as a job candidate than someone who chose a different path.

Another reason a college education has become de rigueur in the workplace is the **shifting focus of the economy** over the last several decades.

There are many of us who can say that we are either the first generation in our families to get a higher education, or that our parents were the first to go to college. Alongside the parental (that'd be me) or recent immigration factor, after the 1950s a fundamental shift in the economy and the job market took place. (Before then, if you could imagine, a high school diploma was all you needed to land yourself a good white-collar job—with a pension, no less!) The glory days of behemoth industry and manufacturing are over. Smarty-pants are in. Popular writer-economist Peter Drucker sums this up by saying we've shifted into a "knowledge economy." The Bureau of Labor Statistics (BLS, a division of the U.S. Department of Labor) more generically calls this a "new economy." In 2001, the BLS reported that the importance of a college education in this "new economy" is made salient by the fact that despite a shrinking college population, there has been a tremendous increase in college enrollments.

Census data show that between 1987 and 1997, the college enrollment of twenty- to twenty-four-year-olds increased 30 percent despite the fact that the actual number of twenty- to twenty-four-year-olds in the country *decreased* by 1.3 million in the same ten years.

Sociologist-economist poobah Professor Richard Florida became very popular recently with his more encompassing stance that not only is the economy knowledge-driven, but it is also—and will continue to be—driven by a combination of knowledge, information, and creativity, fueling a rapidly growing innovation economy. Now, according to Professor Florida, because creativity is valued as much as, if not more than, just knowledge and information on their own, we're heading toward

the formation of two inter-
dependent classes of society:
the "Creative Class" and the
"Service Class."*
Florida states that the problem is that those that are left
behind (non-college-educated)
are going to end up getting
sucked into the Service Class
because the members of the

> **$27,280**
>
> average 2002 earnings by a
> high school graduate
>
> **$51,194**
>
> average 2002 earnings by a
> college graduate

dang Creative Class make so much money and work such long,
encompassing hours that someone is going to have to take care
of all the day-to-day stuff (now, who'd that be?). The more
money we make and the more educated we become, the stronger
the need for a service economy to support us. And so the wheel
turns . . . **Pick a side.**

Another raison d'être for the education push is the upcoming rapid retirement rate of baby boomers. Millions of those
boomers will be retiring in the next ten years, leaving heaps of
empty job slots. Great news! Lots of jobs! But the majority of
these positions **require a college degree.** According to our
friends at the BLS, in the ten-year span from 1998 to 2008
college-level jobs are projected to grow more than 27 percent.
And as the *Occupational Outlook Quarterly* online reported in
2000, "For the first time in years, openings for college-level
jobs are expected to nearly equal the number of college-
educated labor force entrants."

*Check out Professor Florida's awesome (though hefty) tome, *The Rise of
the Creative Class*, Basic Books, 2002.

But it's no time to get lax. The BLS report mentioned above also states that because of this job-exits-equal-job-entries trend, expectations for high salaries and job satisfaction will also increase. This brings about an even more competitive environment not only for the best jobs on the totem pole, but hopefully for employers to satisfy their employees as well.

## THE RISING COSTS OF EDUCATION

*"Universities share one characteristic with compulsive gamblers and exiled royalty: there is never enough money to satisfy their desires."** 

So we've established that to make a good buck in this *grande* land called America, we need at least a college education. And to get this education, what is required of us? Money. Lots of it.

Why does it cost so damn much if it's basically a requirement? We can go to public high schools on our parents' tax dollars because it's required. So why is a college education getting exorbitantly—almost prohibitively—expensive the more we need it?

Well, you can refer to Prof. Bok's dead-on quote above for a quick answer. A bit of a longer, more involved answer is that universities are moneymaking and increasingly commercialized private institutions (even the public ones)—some are even corporations (University of Phoenix, anyone?).

*From Derek Bok, *Universities in the Marketplace: The Commercialization of Higher Education,* Princeton University Press, 2003.

Since the late 1970s, when Pell Grants from the federal government covered up to 84 percent of the costs of a four-year college, the bankrolls and operations of higher education have taken a big, hard right turn. A combo of the feds pulling back on their support of college students and the schools themselves (an energy crisis, crime, and war gobbled up most of the government to-do list in the 1960s and 1970s), universities needing to find alternative funds to support their growth and research (hint: athletics) and a ratcheting up of competition among institutions have created a rising spiral of college costs.

According to CNNMoney.com, the reason tuition costs rose between 4.5 and 11 percent for the 2004–05 school year was a combination of labor costs and health care for staff, student aid (since fewer can afford to go, schools are giving more and more aid—whaaa?), and, as I already mentioned, competition among schools in the battle for the best reputations, best faculties, and best student body (gotta pump out more rich, successful alums).

You can't blame them, really. We've already established that job competition requires higher education levels and training, so universities and colleges are under more pressure than ever to attract top students, athletes, and funding. However, institutions have become so skilled and entrepreneurial in their approach to moneymaking—including corporate sponsorship of research facilities and top students—that they are, for the most part, richer than ever. So again you ask, why the mind-blowing costs?

Well, just how bad is it? (Humor me here.) It got bad enough that in 1998 Congress created an amendment to the Higher Education Act ordering a study of the costs paid by institutions

> **46%**
>
> increase in cost of public college
> tuition in the past five years
> —College Board, 2004

and the prices paid by students. (Just to make sure there wasn't some price gougin' goin' on, no doubt.) The commission that ran this study found that the amount students pay for their college education is increasing faster than inflation (both private and public), and that institution costs are also increasing fast, but not as fast as the payouts made by students.

Our friends at the BLS break it down farther: From 1987 to 1997, the Consumer Price Index for goods and services rose 41 percent, while during the same decade college tuition and fees rose **111 percent!** The U.S. Department of Education reported in 2002 that between 1981 and 2000, in both public and private colleges and universities, the average tuition (adjusted for inflation, of course) more than *doubled,* while the median family income rose only 27 percent in that same time period. Hmm. Quite the gap to close there.

So just at a time where you gotta gotta have that degree, it gets harder and harder to pay for it. And though at least half of students get some or all their tuition paid by their parents and almost a third live at home, too, Mom and/or Dad are becoming less and less likely to help out. Why the tighter wallets? Because parents are living longer and longer, and their retirement accounts got hit hard by the previous recession. Thus, they now have bigger and bigger retirement costs and needs.

So we get resourceful. The Census Bureau says that 75 percent of all full-time college students worked while in college. A staggering 40 percent of these worked full time. (Good Lord— you guys are amazing . . .) The BLS puts this number closer to

30 percent, with 53 percent of students working twenty-five or more hours a week.

But there are only so many hours in a day and for now, self-cloning is prohibitive, so loans are rapidly becoming the number one method of paying for a college education (that's not including the won-

| HOW WE PAY FOR COLLEGE | |
|---|---|
| 1999–'00 | |
| 55% | financial aid |
| 31% | grants |
| 43% | loans |
| 75% | work |

—U.S. Dept. of Ed, 2002;
U.S. Census Bureau, 2002

derfully lucky bunch who just write checks—bah).

Back in the day, the federal government straight up gave money to college students (in the form of grants), but now the government has instead become the biggest lender to college and graduate students. Well, at least they're subsidized loans (see chapter 3 for an explanation of why this is a good thing).

It doesn't really seem to matter too much in dollar amounts due whether you go to public or private schools. Nellie Mae (she probably visits your mailbox every month, or maybe her sister Sallie?) reported in 2003 that the average debt incurred by a graduating four-year college student was $21,200 for private schools and $17,900 for public schools. Yee-ouch.

Let's juxtapose those digits with what Nellie Mae reports as starting salaries after graduation: $26,400 (private) and $26,800 (public).

A moment of silence to digest the shock.

Do I dare even venture into the land of graduate and professional school costs? Heck, as I'm writing this, I've got a super-grand five-figure total for my master's degree. Why not . . .

According again to Ms. Nellie Mae, the average debt a graduate student leaves school with—along with that diploma—is
$45,900. This same graduate student will average a starting
salary of $42,100 a year. That shade of red does not exist in
nature.

It's been awhile now since credit cards have become a substantial way of life for graduate students, even just for day-to-day
expenses. Undergrads have caught on. The average undergrad
now leaves school with $1,843 in credit card debt.

It's a love–hate relationship we have with the debt we incur
for our higher education. The bills are a tremendous burden—
yet without them, we wouldn't have been able to get that degree that got us that well-paying job, right? Quite the Faustian
bargain. But I'll get to show you how to get the upper hand on
this smooth devil called debt soon. Stay tuned.

## INTERNSHIPS: AKA INDENTURED SERVITUDE

Internships. They can be paid or unpaid, a genuine training and
recruiting program, a glorified temp job, or, worst-case scenario,
just another form of indentured servitude. For the most wanted,
*cool* jobs and careers, the latter two types tend to be the norm.

According to the National Association of Colleges and Employers (NACE), in 2004 internships were the top recruiting
method used by employers to find new full-time employees.
The *Financial Times* recently reported that half of U.S. college
graduates hired have gone through internship programs. Some
good news for those on the internship track comes from *Business
Week* online, which says that as we're pulling ourselves out of an

economic slump, the classes of '04 and '05 will get 25 to 35 percent more internship offers than in the past several years, and that the number of full-time job offers after completion of an internship will rise the same amount.

Here's the problem I—and a growing, vocal group of others—have with the practice of internships: They remain fairly unregulated, and many continue to be unpaid (especially in the more creative, hot fields such as publishing and music or film production design).

I had a couple of internships. One in my undergrad years did not pay, but I did get full course credit; a quasi-internship after graduate school barely paid a minimum salary. I'm very glad I had these experiences, and there is no doubt that my undergrad internship was a huge factor in getting my first job out of college. However, as the practice of not paying interns grows, and as it becomes more and more important to have an internship—well, let me relay an anecdote:

Several years ago, I caused quite a ruckus at my ridiculously low-paying post-graduate internship when I walked away from a prestigious offer from the top dog to return instead to the world of earning a fair wage. Thankfully my job switch was a good idea for many reasons, not just because I couldn't pay my rent where I was at, but also because as I walked out, looking behind me, what did I see?

At one of the most prestigious institutions in its field, I did not see behind me the crème de la crème of thinkers, healers, and researchers. No. What I saw was the mediocrity left over from the sieve that is formed by the need to survive at a job and profession that leave you with loans up the wazoo, then pay you near nothing for the internships and fellowships required to even officially enter the career. These folks weren't the best and brightest. They were simply the ones who had parents and/or family who could help them financially survive the process. What a shame.

Writer Laura Vanderkam recently agreed with this in her *USA Today* column on how unpaid or low-paying internships eliminate many of the best-qualified candidates from the hiring pool. The system doesn't get you the best candidates. What you get is the 20 percent or so of the total available candidates whose parents or family are able to bankroll their living expenses. She wrote, "If the interns who would make my life easier are working construction jobs because their parents can't bankroll their unpaid summers doing my research, then I have a problem." Right on, Ms. V.

*The New York Times* chimed in with a piece titled "Crucial Unpaid Internships Increasingly Separate the Haves from the Have-Nots." The article wondered: If it's becoming more and more important to join the workforce not only with an advanced degree, but with an internship in your industry as well, is there a discriminatory class system being created that undermines potential interns from less wealthy families—who have to turn down these unpaid posts for jobs that pay, but may not be where their career interests lie?

And according to the career information web site Vault.com, unpaid internships tend to be most common in the most competitive career slots, such as media and politics. Shoot, even the White House doesn't pay the hundred or more interns who work the halls every summer. And if the White House is basically discriminating in its choice of interns by siphoning out those who can't afford to work for free, where does that leave the other 80 percent of us? (And what kind of elitist roster of Capitol Hill clones does that perpetuate?)

The Fair Labor Standards Act says that employers must pay a minimum wage. However, there is a legal window in the law that says that it's okay not to pay someone who doesn't contribute directly to the company's operations. Now, we all know that that loophole gets stretched.

So employers have an already fairly well-trained pool of potential entry-level employees who are of minimal expense. Meantime a group of potential employees—who want to be there so bad they work for free—know that their chances of getting a full-time post are much higher because their foot was in the door first. Sound like a win–win situation?

That's the bittersweet joy of internships. There is no doubt how important they are, and they do give you invaluable experience (that is, if you use your time there wisely—my advice is, read everything you photocopy, treat everyone with respect, and make yourself indispensable—worked for me). The conundrum is that you may have to work harder to get one that pays, or have to work another job to pay the rent, or, like I did, end up in more debt in the short term.

## THE COMPETITION CHOKE

Workplace competition has become fierce. Our economy has become more global, technologically advanced, and complex, ratcheting up contention in the American job market and workplace. All this fueled by our increasing levels of consumption—supersize me!

| WHO'S GOT A COLLEGE DEGREE? (WORKERS AGE 25 TO 34 WITH A BACHELOR'S OR HIGHER) | | |
|---|---|---|
| | 1992 | 2000 |
| Writer, artist, athlete | 56% | 69% |
| Police, detective | 15% | 24% |
| Farm operator, manager | 13% | 21% |

—U.S. Dept. of Ed., 2002; U.S. Census Bureau, 2002

So we have to work more and harder to pay for the cars, bigger homes, better clothes, electronics, travel, and an upgraded American lifestyle. We have to look good because now more than ever, how you look communicates who you are and what you can deliver. As my mother always said, "Don' dress for de job ju haf. Dress for de job ju want!" Ma was ahead of her time. When you enter the job market and the workforce now, you are a brand—the brand of "me." It's time to sell yourself as the best man/woman for the job. And you must have e-mail access and a cell phone, printer, and Palm Pilot.

Our consumer society creates a battle for the best-paying jobs, and an education becomes just one facet in the package of "you." As the economist Pierre Bourdieu stated years ago, **cultural capital**—which consists of not just level of education but also family upbringing and economic resources—is indispensable in order to get ahead in the workplace. We live in a time when it's increasingly important not only to get the best education, but also to consume well. Levels of taste and consumption create distinctions in the workplace that add a very difficult and sometimes unfair measure of how far you'll go in life. We take our economic, cultural, and social capital and compete in the workplace.

For example, as we all know, if you have two job candidates equal on paper, but one is more likely to look, act, and speak smoothly and well at a client dinner—knowing which wine to choose, what branzino is, and how long it takes to fly to Shanghai—this guy or gal is probably going to be the one to get the job.

Writer Stuart Ewen noted back in 1988 that style has become a sort of "legal tender." Because we live in a land of marketing, packaging, advertising, and democracy, we've created a very real pressure to have an image, a personal brand. We don't distinguish ourselves just by our accomplishments but very prominently by our appearance. Nice packaging is the American way.

So you graduate from college in debt but then need to have the latest equipment—cell phone, laptop, BlackBerry—and look great while interviewing and on the job, and again, how does all this get paid for? Just one generation back, young adults were still using typewriters and everyone simply had a land line. Now it's a grand or so for a good computer, plus internet access, a cell phone, and an organizer. You're already in the hole for another $2,000 and you haven't even shopped for your interview outfit.

Getting a job is a form of competition, and the standards of this competition have only gotten higher and harder, with no signs of slowing down.

## MEMO TO CREDITORS: STOP THROWING MONEY AT US!

So how's a young upstart to pay for all this stuff?

BankFirst now has an Usher debit MasterCard. There's a Hilary Duff card, too. Who would want a credit or debit card with the face of their favorite pop star on it? Even better, Visa now lets you put your *own* face on your credit card, or any other picture

you'd like. (Ah, the ultimate brand promotion—you!) Disproportionately, it's young people who are interested in these cus-
tom jobs. Junior Achievement says that 13 percent of teens age
thirteen to eighteen have credit cards now. Teenagers barely
know how to manage cash, let alone a credit card. But that
doesn't stop credit card companies from approving lines of
credit to someone too young to have a job.

As you're all too aware, college campuses are huge credit
card recruitment centers, with sign-up kiosks all over campuses
and credit offers stuffed in mailboxes. Creditors are eager to
get you started borrowing early and young, and they know that
college is probably the best place to begin. Bank of America has
a "CampusEdge" debit card that can be linked to a credit line
that offers monthly fees for only the first six months, or free for
five years if a parent has an account.

They just keep making it easier and easier to borrow money.
And what a growing amount of money it is.

CardData reported in late 2004 that in the month of July,
$5.6 billion was added to the total of revolving credit Ameri-
cans have, most of it in credit card debt. That's compared with
$1 billion a year ago.

## THE STIGMA IS GONE:
## WHY BIG DEBT HAS BECOME THE NORM

Debt has been normalized. Everyone has it, right? So what's the
big deal?

Now, who do you think makes money off promoting the idea
that debt is okay? That it's a normal part of life? Well, banks

make money off lenders and borrowers, credit card companies make money all around, stores, too—any store, actually, since debt tends to occur when you buy something—the government, the stock market, the hospitality business, and on and on. And heck, the economy in general goes up when we spend, so maybe it's in everyone's best interest but our own?

Do you remember a weird time after 9/11 when the buzz out of Washington was that if you were not out spending, spending, spending, you were being almost un-American? We were told to go on vacation, buy clothes, eat out, and stock up. It was bizarre. Instead of the usual sacrifices asked of Americans during unstable times in the past, we were asked to support America by spending money. And for most of us, it's money that we don't have.

What kind of culture supports such a seemingly backward and potentially crippling way of life for its citizens? A consumer culture.

When did America become such a culture of consumers? Well, according to Lendol Calder in his 1999 book *Financing the American Dream: A Cultural History of Consumer Credit,* before the 1920s the practices of installment payments and loans to make purchases were not held in high esteem. The popularization of the automobile changed a lot of that. Detroit knew that it had to sell cars on credit since they were too expensive for most of the population. Pre-1920s, America was being told by critics that it was promoting "consumptive" behavior. But soon enough, that word with all its negative connotations (tuberculosis used to be called *consumption*) was changed by marketers and economists to the bright and shiny *consumer.* In a conflagration of events stemming from banking, Wall Street, Detroit, the government, and the Depression, mounds and mounds of consumer debt was encouraged all around. Consumer debt not only became something to be unembarrassed about, but almost became the norm. Who are we kidding? It *is* the norm!

How many people do you know who don't have any debt of any kind? I'm thinking your answer is close to zero. Me too. When a rite of adult passage is getting a credit card, you're backward for not having the latest tech gadget, and entry-level pay is lower than it was in the 1970s (adjusted for inflation), we've come to a time and place where debt has lost its stigma.

Extensive debt is a way of life. If it's everywhere and nearly everyone's got it—we're all living beyond our means—why fix it?

Because too often, it hurts. Because it squeezes and wrings until your hard-earned money is unable to breathe, or even see the light of day. Because as you're teetering on that precipice of losing what you have and just squeaking by, it doesn't feel good—it makes you tired. If debt is not managed well, it can become your prison. But if you take control of your situation as soon as you can, you can prevent that multiple-year sentence for overspending. Instead you have every power to nip it in the bud, start up new and better habits, and actually maybe *enjoy* that raise you got this year.

Best of all, soon again, you'll be able to breathe.

## Web Links

**generationdebt.org** The original "Generation Debt" site, with information, blog, and commentary on the state of young people and debt.

**maxedoutgen.com** Another good site to commiserate with other young folks in debt.

**gao.gov** The official web site of the Government Accountability Office, it studies how the federal government spends taxpayer dollars.

**villagevoice.com** An alternative web site for New York City and the nation: news, features, fashion, gossip, arts, opinions, classifieds, personals, entertainment listings, restaurant reviews.

**bls.gov** The site of the U.S. government's Bureau of Labor Statistics, with more info on workers in America.

**ed.gov** The U.S. Department of Education web site, with good info for students on financial aid, research and statistics, and many other programs.

**nelliemae.com** The site for our government-lending lady friend Nellie Mae, with info on loans, money management, and more.

**vault.com** A job information site with career services, job management, and company information.

**monstertrak.com** An info-based web page for the job-hunting site Monster.com, with connections for students to employers and career centers.

**internships.com** Find and apply for internships in multiple fields, and get more info on your rights.

**money.com** Info from *Money* magazine on cars, real estate, personal finance, and many other areas to help you in building your future.

**businessweek.com** The *Business Week* magazine site with the latest news, investing tips, business schools, and a career section.

# Get a Grip. Set Goals. Make a Plan.

## *Take Control*

We've all heard the tale of the $3.50 latte. (Groan.)

How if you'd just cut back on a couple of those a week, you could have an additional $35 or more a month. Easier said than done, especially when a latte may be the only indulgence a tight budget allows. But maybe there is a cheaper way to indulge?

And do you really need an MP3 player—right now? Or can you survive another three months with that iPod? How about that extra appetizer or drink? Maybe if you're still hungry (or thirsty), you can wait to fill up cheaply when you get home.

## IDENTIFYING NEEDS VS. WANTS

On a limited income, needs and wants require stricter definitions and, sometimes, a rather agonizing dividing line. But tallying up a list of your own needs vs. wants is a good start to getting a grip on the drip, drip of a leaky, "Where does my money go?" financial faucet.

Here's a short box set to start you thinking about your own **needs vs. wants.** I've filled in a couple of lines with some of my own to get your personal finance juices flowin':

| Needs | Wants |
|---|---|
| apartment | iPod |
| weekly subway pass | laptop upgrade |
| cell phone service | dining out 4 times a week |
| web access | cab rides |

Now, you may need that newspaper subscription to your local paper so you're informed of the goings-on in town, but do you really need that $4.99 glossy interior design or Euro car magazine off the newsstand? Will you survive without it?

Yes, you will survive. Even better, you'll have contributed toward saving for your new iPod. Awesome . . . And catch yourself rationalizing your behavior, flipping "wants" into the "needs" box. That, my friends, is a self-sabotaging no-no.

Another *dinero* distinction that will help fine-tune your needs vs. wants list is to understand how your spending breaks down into **fixed vs. flexible expenses.** Some bills and expenses are the same every month, while others allow for some wiggle room.

Your rent or mortgage payment is likely the same every month, as are your phone bill, probably your energy bill, and maybe transportation—and all these are needs. Basically, your monthly bills are, for the most part, your fixed expenses. Your trips to the salon or barbershop, your chick-lit or *manga* book habit, CDs, and (legal) downloading are all flexible expenses.

Getting a picture of how these items fit into your expenses will show you how much you have left for flexible expenses, savings, and fun money. Here's a fixed expenses list to get started:

### Fixed expenses (monthly)

| | |
|---|---|
| rent/mortgage | $_____ |
| electric/gas bill | _____ |
| heating/AC bill | _____ |
| water bill | _____ |
| land-line phone service | _____ |
| cell phone service | _____ |
| web access | _____ |
| transportation: public | _____ |
|    car payment | _____ |
|    gas | _____ |
|    tolls | _____ |
|    car insurance | _____ |
| student loans | _____ |
| credit cards | _____ |
| health insurance/costs | _____ |
| **TOTAL:** | $_____ |

Next, tally up your flexible expenses costs (wants). This is where you can try to cut down, cut out, or trade off on your wallet outlay. And this time, let's look at costs per week to be more precise—multiply the total by 4 for a monthly total:

## Flex Expenses (weekly)

| | |
|---|---|
| breakfast/coffee | $_____ |
| lunches | _____ |
| dinner out | _____ |
| after-work drinks | _____ |
| groceries | _____ |
| taxis | _____ |
| music/books/magazines | _____ |
| movies/DVDs | _____ |
| dry cleaning/laundry | _____ |
| drug store/cosmetics | _____ |
| clothes/shoes/accessories | _____ |
| pet(s)/hobbies | _____ |
| **TOTAL:** | $_____ |

Now you can also add up all those pop-up expenses such as birthday presents, travel to visit family and friends, that annual vacation, and car or home repair, and estimate how much you spend on these items each year. **Divide by 12** for an idea of the monthly cost of these extra expenses.

## FINAL ROUND IN THE BATTLE OF EXPENSES VS. INCOME

You're almost there. Now, how much do you pull in a month, after taxes? Let's see how all your expenses subtract from your monthly income. Do you come out in the red, in the black, or straight even in the end?

**Monthly income:**                              $_____

___ total fixed bills:                              _____

___ total flex expenses:                          _____

___ total extra expenses:                        _____

=

**What you have left each month**          $_____

So do you have any money left? Or did you end up with a negative number? If so, don't despair. Just seeing in black and white where your money is going is the first step in getting a grip on it.

The next step is to understand (and yes, believe) that you can make some changes with your flexible expenses and those surprising little extras that sometimes take big chunks out of your wallet or, worse, credit card.

## DELAYED GRATIFICATION AND THE B-WORD

There's nothing wrong with having a mantra now and then, especially one that keeps you in a beneficial state of mind.

How about getting comfortable and confident with the words **delayed gratification**? When you pick up that new CD or shirt or sneakers, ask yourself: *Do I really need this right now? Really, really, truly? Can I do without it? Can I wait?*

You'd be surprised at how many things you put down and don't take to the register when you say those words. And the potential cost of each of these items can go toward either something you need, or a goal you have. Bottom line: What's in your wallet stays intact.

Now, there is no need to inform your friends and co-workers about your growing intimacy with the next word: **budget.** There is no shame in the B-word, but there is resistance and a sniff of frugality about it. Budgeting seems tight-ass, but it's actually quite freeing. It frees you from the shackles of debt and financial despair, my friends.

And you may be surprised to find that there is much satisfaction in successful self-control. You'll love yourself in the morning.

So stand tall with your B-word (and yes, I'll keep it among ourselves) and let's get on with how it's done.

The beginning of this chapter got you on the first track of budgeting: knowing where you spend your money now. Here are the next steps on the budget trail to help get you to where you need to be:

- Hook yourself up with **financial software** (such as Quicken) to help keep track of your expenses. These packages have built-in budget-making tools to personalize your budget. If you don't want to spring for the cost of software, set up a spreadsheet yourself to keep a monthly tally and do some basic math.
- **Pay cash!** Okay, that may not be reasonable for every transaction, but if you leave your credit cards and debit cards at home when you go out, you'll be much less likely to get into budget trouble. Also, try to stick to a set cash amount every week and limit yourself to it—when it's gone, it's gone!

- Take special note of your ATM withdrawals. Those late-night visits to the local convenience store ATM can eat up $2.50 a shot—$1.50 to the convenience store or mall and $1.00 to your bank. **Stick to your bank's ATMs.** And if you're visiting the money machine more than twice a week, step back and look again where your cash is going.

- **Keep track** of where your cash bleeds out—say, those lattes or lunches with your work buddies. Cut or reduce those items and watch the bottom line of your budget get rosy.

- Ever hear of the word *tithe*? If you come from a churchgoing family, you probably have. Its dictionary definition involves giving 10 percent of your income to the church. In this case, **let's tithe ourselves,** shall we? Try living off only 90 percent of your take-home income—work from that amount. Let the other 10 percent disappear from your mind—though where it actually ends up is in your bank account.

- Be careful of potential money coming in such as your tax return or a bonus. Don't plan against it and spend it before it gets to you. These **gains** should be dealt with as

they come and divvied out as best you can across your existing bills and savings.

- Watch out for raises and promotions. That couple extra
  thou doesn't work out to that much bi-weekly. Try not to
  get a jump up on your raises. Be happy and proud, but try
  to make those **pay increases** work for you with more
  going to savings or bill paying. Don't adjust your lifestyle
  to a raise until you can operate in the black.

## DO YOUR DEAL HOMEWORK

In this day of rebates, constant sales, online bargain shopping,
and outlets, there is almost never a reason to pay retail—ever!
You're always on the computer anyway, so why not use your
technology access powers for good? Become a much-envied
**master of the deal.**

Everybody spends, but only the best know how to get
exactly the same products and services for less. And really, with
all the tools at our fingertips for mastering the game of "shop,"
there is no excuse for not trying to win every chance you get.

Let's start with some expenses where a little research can go
a long way. (I'll list web links at the end of this chapter—and
every chapter—to make this process easier.)

### PHONE COMPANIES
They are going crazy competing against each other. Especially
now that most also provide land-line service for a dial-up internet connection, or DSL service packages. And now there are
companies such as Vonage that are offering unlimited calls over

your high-speed internet cable for one monthly charge. Take advantage of this pricing war and switch your phone company, and keep switching until you've got the best deal out there.

## CELL PHONES

These have become quite the necessity. Heck, you may not even need that land line at all (especially if your internet connection is cable-based). And now that **you can carry your cell phone number with you** when you switch providers, the only thing stopping you from getting the best deal is that darn contract you signed.

If you are stuck with a cell phone service contract, go to your provider's web site and see what deals it has going. Many cell phone companies break out new packages every other month or so to stay competitive. You may be able to **improve your current plan**—but speak to a representative so you don't get locked into another annual contract, unless you're confident it's one of the best deals out there.

## INTERNET ACCESS

Another necessity. But just like cell phones, once you're out of a contract (or hopefully haven't locked yourself into a bad one in the first place), you can use low-cost or no-cost providers such as **Netzero** or **Earthlink** for better deals on this monthly expense.

## SHOPPING

Buying anything these days can be a deal quest. Shoot, many folks love to compete to see who can pay the least for something. It's a great quirk to have. Shop the major sales at bargain retailers.

Are you near a city where there are sample sales for designer goods? Get online and check out their schedule. Troll for great secondhand items on your local **Craigslist.com** or flea markets and garage sales. Thrift is in.

And with the fantastic auction behemoth known as **eBay,** everything from electronics to washing machines to designer clothes can be had at less (or much, much less) than 50 percent of its retail price. And large retailers frequently dump their overstock on eBay, so be sure to check out their **eBay stores.**

Experienced advice for eBay shoppers:

> ### RETAIL SALE SEASONS
>
> **January:** Almost everything!— winter clothes, boots, accessories, housewares, and linens.
>
> **February/March:** Sweaters, outlet store clearances.
>
> **April:** Sheets, spring clothes.
>
> **July/August:** Sheets, bedding, summer clothes, and accessories.
>
> **September:** Jeans.
>
> **October:** Suits.
>
> **November/December:** Gloves, scarves, tablewares, pre-holiday sales.

- For big-ticket items, make sure the seller has a feedback rating at 95 percent or better, and note how many transactions the seller has completed.
- Keep transactions U.S.-based, if possible, and be responsible about paying promptly for the auctions you win.

And when you're paying retail, why not have the web do your **comparison shopping** for you? There are great sites that allow you to comparison-shop everything from used cars to the latest hardcover fiction, digital cameras to Pumas.

Again, when you're shopping on comparison sites such as **bizrate.com** and **mysimon.com,** make sure to note their product ratings and customer ratings of the retailer. Shipping with some retailers can be slow. In that case, you might want to pay just a bit more to another vendor so you can get your new MP3 in time for the long icky bus ride to your brother's house.

## AUTOMATE, AUTOMATE, AUTOMATE

I find this to be one of the most revolutionary lifestyle developments in years: the ability to **automate banking** and **pay bills online.**

Awhile ago, I closed a checking and savings account with a bank I had been with for years. Why? Because those fools were charging me $10 a month for having a checking balance below their seemingly arbitrary minimum (not to mention that having more than that amount in a checking account at one time is foolish—it should be somewhere else, earning interest!). They were also charging me 35 cents for each check I wrote. Plus a dollar on every ATM withdrawal that wasn't at their machines. And I had direct deposit with these guys!

Well, I may have been slow (or lazy) to join the bandwagon, but doing all your banking online is not only an incredibly sound and secure financial decision, but tremendously cheap as well.

You save on monthly banking fees (usually with direct deposit of your paycheck), check-writing fees, and sometimes ATM fees. Can we just think about getting rid of the pain of finding and buying stamps for a moment? Amazing.

So wait no longer. Go to your bank of choice (look for very

low or no monthly fees) and open an account that you can manage online. For a listing of various banks and their online capabilities and fees, go to **bankrate.com** for a comparison.

Many large banks offer great deals—I'm saving a good $16 to $20 a month from the switch—and the differences tend to be in web navigation convenience and branch locations. But most banks waive monthly maintenance fees when you bank online. After all, they're saving money on check processing every time someone pays a bill online. The Federal Reserve recently estimated that it costs banks $1 to $5 to put through a written check, while an online payment costs them as little as 7 cents. A win–win situation.

You can also automate your bill payments by signing up with your utility or student loan companies: Visit their web site or give them a call to sign up for automatic bill pay. If you have a consistent income, this can be a way to build up excellent credit—you'll never have to worry about missing payments or being late on a bill.

If you're tight on cash, however, this may not be a good idea. There are months when waiting a few extra days to send a payment (though still on time!) can save you from overdrawing your checking account. Wait until you know you can handle the automatic withdrawals.

Another cost-cutting strategy to work out with the bank you choose is to apply for overdraft protection. When I started out after undergrad, I automatically signed up for overdraft protection when I opened my local checking account. And even though I wasn't making that much money, I had a decent credit history and ended up qualifying for protection. It was worth it when I once misjudged a payment schedule and came up short for a bill (my rent!). But I was covered and never bounced a check—ever. The interest rates on overdraft accounts are super-high, so make sure that if you use your overdraft protection you pay it off right away. It's for emergencies only—not a cash account to go shopping on. Used wisely, never bouncing a check again can save you $30-plus each time.

Many companies, such as Sallie Mae and Con Edison, would love you to sign up for bill paying on their web sites. But I think it's a pretty big pain in the butt to have to visit several sites to pay several different bills. With your bank ready and able to send out payments to anyone you want online, why bother with multiple sites? Stick to either paying your bills with automatic withdrawals or—more likely and more appealing to me—pay your bills online from your bank's web site. It's secure, it's fast, and with many banks you can set up an automatic payment to any payee you'd like as well.

Remember, though, that while the bank withdraws the money for a bill you pay automatically, the payment may not reach its destination for a couple of days. Still, with everything going electronic these days—including the scanning and transmission of paper checks—mailing times will get shorter. Soon payments will go out and be received within a day. For now, though, keep on top of what the receiving date is for your online bill payments and factor that in when setting up payments.

Some banks charge fees for online banking—as I write, these range from $6.95 at Wachovia to $5.00 at Washington Mutual—but with so many banks out there realizing that users of online banking cost much less to them than regular branch bankers, those fees are being waived. Free online banking will soon be the norm. Do your best to search out the best bank with the best online bill-payment setup.

## CREATING AND STICKING TO A MASTER PLAN

Okay, you've got a budget going, and you've shopped around for the best deals on your essentials and other purchases. Now you ask me the James Lipton question: "What's my motivation?" **Your goals,** my friends. Your goals.

Having small goals, such as trying out that nouveau Pan-Asian joint on Saturday night with your new girlfriend or boyfriend, or larger goals, such as getting a graduate degree or vacationing in the Caribbean, can motivate you to be financially responsible and savvy in ways you've yet to dream.

Setting goals and sticking to a plan gives you a vision to keep in your head when that latte/gin-and-tonic/pair of shoes calls you to buy. It enables you to "just say no." But we all have goals, some more amorphous than others, so focus is needed. Here are some tips on solid goal making and setting your priorities:

- When it comes to finances, you've got to **concentrate.** You may not be able to have both a vacation and a new work wardrobe this year. Which do you want more? Or is there a third goal that can be eliminated so you can have goals number one and two? If you hook yourself into a smaller but well-thought-out set of goals, you have a better chance of achieving them.
- **Pop-up expenses** happen. No doubt one week you'll be asked to a baby shower (pop-up number one) and a bridal shower (pop-up number two), and you'll need new contact lenses at the same time (pop-up number three). These things *can* be manageable. Be creative and frugal where you can (with the gifts) while spending on what you

really need (those contact lenses). It helps if you keep a small cushion of cash in your bank account to always cover those unexpected yet forever-popping-up expenses.

- When laying out goals, make sure to look at the **time frame.** If you're thinking about saving for a down payment on a house, how much time are you giving yourself? By setting up a reasonable (and realistic) schedule to complete your financial goals, you'll be able to determine your priorities and budget for other items with longer lead times.
- **Set yourself up right.** Make sure *you* are happy and secure before you work to make anyone else happy. Include an emergency fund into your budgeting goals that can cover you for at least three months without a paycheck. And do your best to take care of debt before getting in any deeper.
- **Get started, pronto.** Now it's time to get moving on your money goals, budget, and plans. The sooner you get started, the more rewards you'll reap. And if you're having trouble getting started, do what they tell writers to do when paralyzed by inertia: Sit in front of the computer (or piece of paper) and just start.
- **Don't beat yourself up.** Look, we all mess up once in a while. Sometimes you just have to have that freakin' latte or you'll go mad. But learn from the glitches in your plan and get back on course. Ask yourself if what you're spending is taking you closer to happiness (an A-plus on your budget!) or quickening your debt descent.

Great job. Take a bow. You've joined me in the land of budgets, goals, and savvy spending. Or at least I've inspired you to make the first step. Keep going, *amigo,* we're on the right track.

## Web Links

**sidestep.com** A comprehensive site for price comparison of online travel sites.

**pricegrabber.com** This is a good comparison-shopping site for everything from clothes to mortgages, music, art, software, and gaming.

**bizrate.com** Fast comparison shopping with more than forty thousand stores.

**shopzilla.com** A very user-friendly comparison shopping site.

**lowermybills.com** Find lower prices for your phone service, cell phone, internet access, insurance, loans, and credit cards.

**swapagift.com** Got a gift certificate or gift card from the Moms, but don't like the store? Visit here to swap it for another store's card and pay a flat $3.99 for the exchange.

---

### OTHER WEB LINKS

| **Cash Flow & Budgeting** | **Decor** | **Phone Service** |
|---|---|---|
| money.cnn.com | target.com | att.com |
| quicken.com | ikea.com | sprint.com |
| msnmoney.com | urbn.com | mci.com |
| youcandealwithit.com | spiegel.com | verizon.com |

| **Comparison Shopping** | **Travel** | **Internet Service** |
|---|---|---|
| mysimon.com | orbitz.com | netzero.com |
| nextag.com | expedia.com | earthlink.com |
|  | priceline.com |  |
| **And Of Course** | lowestfare.com |  |
| ebay.com | jetblue.com |  |
|  | cheaptickets.com |  |
|  | smarterliving.com |  |

CHAPTER

# 3

# Master Your Student Loans

### *Tame the Beast*

One day—a day like any other—you open your mailbox and flip through the usual junk mail solicitations and trendy catalogs when suddenly, eh, what's this? 'Tis the glaring white envelope holding your first student loan bill.

Six months ago, that diploma—undergrad, graduate, law school, med school—was in your hands. You were proud. Accomplished. And ready to begin an exciting career. Quite the feeling . . .

So you got that job and started settling into the daily grind. Then, months later (if you're lucky), you got a bill—a big bill. The biggest bill you've yet to see: your student loan. Your bank account wails like a pissy toddler and your face resembles *The Scream*.

But didn't these loans help you get to where you are now? Yep, they did . . . Though according to the 2003 National Student Loan Survey (NASLS), that doesn't keep snuggly at night the

55.5 percent of you who report feeling burdened by your student loan payments. Then again, 70 percent of this group agree that getting student loans made it possible to go to college. So let's accept the fact that the necessary evil of student loans can be an indispensable tool in the game called "getting ahead." Accept their existence, find out everything you can on how to manage them well. Then pay those suckers off.

## TYPES OF EDUCATION LOANS, THE RULES OF ENGAGEMENT, AND YOUR RIGHTS AS A BORROWER

First off, being clear about what kind of student loan or loans you have puts you in the best position to manage your debt and keep your interest rates and penalties down.

The most important distinction between the various types of student loans is between **private loans** and **government-backed loans.**

When you borrow from the government (aka federal education loan programs), you get a short break on paying interest at the start of the loan. Also, with these loans, you don't need someone to co-sign for you (a parent, for example). The feds also back these loans so you will get your money no matter what's happening with the economy.

Private, non-G-man loans usually require a co-signer, and interest gets charged right away. And you're screwed if something bad happens to the bank lending you the money—since these loans are not guaranteed, you can be left high and dry of funds if the bank runs into trouble and has its assets seized or frozen (very rare, but a legit concern when dealing with a smaller lender).

Let's start with a breakdown of the two different ways the **government** loans money to you, more commonly known as **Stafford Loans:**

$137%

increase in volume of student loans in the past decade

—*Wall Street Journal,*
October 20, 2004

- **Subsidized loans** are need-based only. The feds pay the interest on the loan while you're in school and during the initial post-graduation grace period. These loans have great—but variable—interest rates.
- **Unsubsidized loans** are open to all takers. Interest starts up at the loan inception, and the lendee is responsible for paying all interest.

KNOW THIS:

There are two kinds of fees placed on many loans that you can negotiate down or get waived.

Origination fees
(around 3% of original loan)

Administrative fees
(1% or so of original loan)

Never hurts to ask . . .

Your school can also lend you money as an undergrad with a **Perkins Loan.** These loans have great deals on fixed interest rates and extended grace periods of up to nine months after you graduate. Take it if you can get it.

**Private loans** can be helpful in a bind, but they're tough to manage and expensive. They're more often used for financing graduate school or continuing education. Instead of owing either of the Mae sisters (Nellie or Sallie—the big federal student loan companies), you may end up owing Citibank, Chase, MBNA, another bank, or your local credit union branch—whoever you borrow from. Interest on these loans starts up right away, and there are no grace periods—if you take out a private bank loan, you can get a bill as soon as you graduate, and interest has already started piling up. Interest rates on private loans can be competitive, but if you're late on even one payment,

> ### COST BREAKDOWN OF A STUDENT LOAN:
> - Borrowed amount
> - Origination fee
> - Accrued interest
> - Administration fee
> - Late fees (Don't do it!)
> - And sometimes an insurance fee

interest and penalties can be jacked up fast and hard.

Basically, a private bank loan is very similar to a really big credit card bill. Ugh.

## PAYBACK OPTIONS AND WHAT TO DO IF YOU CAN'T PAY

I can't believe that I've actually heard people say, "Oh, you don't have to pay back student loans!" *Ig-nor-ant.* Not paying your student loans can unleash ridiculous damage on your credit score (see the next chapter for why this score is so important). This can prevent you from getting a credit card, buying a home, even getting a job.

Maybe back in the day when the government was more likely to pay outright for our college education with grants, and government loans were the new deal on the block, lenders were more lax about repayment. Now, however, rules put into effect by Congress in 2005 make it much easier for lenders to go after student loan deadbeats, and they do, fiercely. The truth is that

> **NOTE:**
>
> If you don't contact your lender *before* you start falling behind in payments, you may not be eligible for forbearance or deferment.

the steady repayment of student loans sets up a great credit record, while nonpayment can result in the garnishing of wages (that'd be when money is taken directly out of your paycheck to pay a debt). However, the government (again, that'd be Sallie or Nellie Mae) understands that it's hard to get a job out of college or grad school these days that can pay for a roof over your head, let alone a monthly bill for $100 or more. They will work with you to make sure you're not overly burdened by loan bills—as long as you make the effort to communicate your situation to them.

The biggest mistake you can make as a borrower (outside of not paying your loan) is not making a simple call to your lender to ask for a different payment plan, or payment amount. These guys want their money back—with interest—and know that it's better to work around your constraints than lose you altogether, or contract your debt out to a loan stalker. (That's my term for collection agencies that come after you via phone, mail, your paycheck, or bank account, armed with the right to get money back, whether you're cooperative or not.)

Let's say you're not able to pay part of your student loan bill, or the whole thing, at any time. Here are some options that you can work out with your lender, with appropriate loan lingo:

### DEFERMENT

If you need to postpone your loan payments for a while, because you're out of work or going back to school, you can potentially qualify to put off (defer) your loan payments for a period of time. However, you have to meet certain requirements of the lender. (Wanting to pay off a huge credit card bill instead of your loan does not make you eligible for deferment.)

The caveat when it comes to deferment is that if your loan is unsubsidized, it will continue to build up interest that you're responsible for paying. If you're lucky enough to have a subsidized loan, you will not be charged interest during this period.

### FORBEARANCE

If you're not able to make loan payments but don't qualify for a deferment, you can put your loan into forbearance. This is an option if, say, you have a medical emergency that puts you out of work, or your monthly student loan bills are more than 20 percent of your monthly income. In forbearance, your loan payments are either postponed for a period of time or reduced to fit your ability to repay.

### PRICIER REPAYMENT OPTIONS OF LAST RESORT

- An **income-sensitive plan** involves loan payments based on the reported income on your tax return. This plan can make your loan take longer to repay (especially if you're paid in nonreported tips or other cash), and your lender has access to all your income reports—there's no escape and little privacy. (You really don't want a lender to know about every raise or bonus you get and then take a piece without asking, do you?)

- Rather than pay your loan over the originally agreed-upon ten-year (less or more) pay period, an **extended repayment plan** lets you negotiate to pay the loan over a longer period, such as twenty years. This may keep you out of defaulting on your loan, but it costs much more in interest.

- With a **graduated repayment plan,** when you first leave school your monthly loan bill will be at its lowest. This bill will then rise along with your income, year after year. Unfortunately, again, you risk paying back the loan

> **WORDS:**
>
> **principal**
> the original amount you borrowed.
>
> **interest**
> what you owe the lender for the privilege of borrowing its money.

and interest over many, many more years. You'll also be required to report your income every year.

There is one more repayment option that allows you to pull together all your loans under one lender's roof for a longer repayment period, but at a lower interest rate. This is a personal friend of mine: **consolidation.**

## How to Consolidate, Again and Again, Pronto

Many personal finance gurus argue against consolidating student loans. In my experience as a once struggling graduate, though, it can prove a mighty useful tool when you've got loans to pay and a low income at an internship or entry-level job. Consolidation of your loans also does not reflect even a smidgen as bad on your credit history as do forbearance or other ways of extending your loans.

A consolidation is basically a refinancing of your existing loan. You buy another loan to cover all your loans, extend the repayment time period, and get a much lower fixed interest rate.

Shaving a couple of percentage points off your student loan means much lower monthly payments.

Again, yes, the repayment period is extended, and the loan can be more expensive in the end than your original loan. However, if that means being able to pay your bill on time, so be it. Take advantage, and when your income grows, up your monthly payment on your own. Remember, you won't be penalized for paying off your loan earlier and faster. Doing this takes care of the "expensive" part—it cancels out the difference. And yes, we're assuming discipline here.

There is also an advantage in consolidating your loan to get a *fixed* interest rate—many loans have variable rates that can make your monthly payment fluctuate. A fixed rate makes your loan predictable and constant. Again, however, you pay for this convenience, so don't forget to up your payment amounts as your income rises.

If you consolidate with Sallie or Nellie Mae, you are still privy to getting discounts if you pay consistently and on time. After four years of a perfect repayment schedule, you can get up to another 1 percent shaved off your interest rate. With a 6 or 8 percent interest rate, that 1 percent is a tremendous discount over the life of the loan.

Now, the *con* of consolidation is not just the extra expense due to the extended loan life. Unfortunately, consolidation may cause you to lose the ability to defer your loan or go into forbearance. And if you consolidate your loans before graduation, you've lucked out of the six- to nine-month grace period—you have to start paying your loan right away (so if you're going to consolidate, wait until after the grace period).

Right now interest rates are incredibly low, so consolidating your loans now could fix an interest rate so good, you'd be set for years. However, should interest rates rise and you consolidate when rates are higher, you're stuck with the rate you get even if rates go down—way down.

One more *con* of consolidation is the possibility of losing your right to cancel your loan. *Cancel?* you say. *How in Vishnu's name can I cancel my student loan?* Well, most loan-cancel options are extreme and not pleasant, but there is one that rewards you in more ways than one.

### STUDENT LOAN CANCELLATION SCENARIOS

- **Die.** Morbid thought, but at least your family won't be responsible for your student loan debt if you pass away.
- Become **permanently disabled** and unable to work. Another very sad thought, but at least you won't have to worry about this bill in addition to everything else.
- Join the **U.S. military.** Well, if you're going to serve your country and risk your life, damn straight you should get those loans taken care of.
- Become the victim of a **school scam.** There are a lot of suspect schools popping up out there. Should you make the mistake of signing up for one and borrowing money to pay for it, you can get your loan canceled if the school shuts down while you're enrolled or you find out your diploma is bogus.
- Get a job **teaching in an inner-city school or working with an underserved community.** This has restrictions and requirements, but it's wonderful to know that if you decide to teach in a low-income urban area, you can put your student loan to rest.

## GRADUATE SCHOOL?

The days of graduate school being a tried-and-true way of making it are not necessarily over, but graduate school is certainly not the sure thing it used to be. The stock market fall of the late 1990s and early 2000s created much heartbreak for MBAs. And with the average cost of a master's degree now up to $40,000, going to graduate school is not something to take lightly.

Graduate or professional school—such as medical school, dental school, and law school—is a big load to take on by yourself, but if what you want to do and be in life requires an advanced degree, those piles and piles of loans may be worth every penny. And there is no doubt that the more education you have, the higher your income. A master's degree can reap you an average of over $25,000 more in annual income than a bachelor's degree alone. That adds up and makes your degree pay for itself in only two or three years. And we all know that once doctors and lawyers get past the first few years of low resident and clerk salaries, they can be assured of high incomes, mostly in the six-figure range.

But graduate school debt is just as bad a problem as undergrad—if not worse. Nellie Mae reports that the average grad school enrollee finishes studies owing about $38,000. There are few grants and scholarships for those looking to get master's degrees. You get more financial aid and scholarships when you're going for a PhD—where you also work like crazy for the university, teaching and researching. Schools want to make sure they get their aid money back by working you hard in return. But there's no doubt that if you thought paying for undergrad (where you were more likely to get help from parents and family) was hard, grad school is a feat.

You'll have many of the same financing options for graduate school as you had for undergraduate: subsidized and unsubsidized student loans. Do your best to take out government-backed loans rather than those from a private lender. With government loans, you'll have more leeway with working out payment schedules and consolidations than with private, bank loans. The rules of borrowing for undergraduate loans that we ran through before hold pretty steady for grad school. But your bills will be much, much bigger.

Paying for graduate school is certainly not impossible, though, and—as I can tell you personally—the huge student loan bills (and credit card bills) you'll rack up extending your education will reap you better job prospects and higher salaries in the long run.

The worst mistake that graduates of professional schools and master's programs make is getting so pumped up at their new high-salaried jobs that they start living the high life before they can afford it. That sudden six-figure salary really isn't a six-figure salary once you factor in how much you'll be paying in student loans a month. When you graduate, take a short vacation, then get back to living the life you had before until you can get those loans down to a manageable figure and your salary high enough to pay for a higher quality of life.

The best reason to go to graduate school is not because you don't know what you want to do in life and your mom would love for you to be a lawyer. Go to graduate school because you love what you'll be studying and/or you need it for your much-desired career. You'll have the best chances of making it, and making it well.

## Web Links

**salliemae.com**  The nation's leading provider of education funding, Sallie Mae's site offers a copious amount of information and resources for students, parents, and financial aid professionals.

**nelliemae.com**  The site for our government-lending lady friend Nellie Mae, with info on loans, money management, and more.

**ed.gov/directloan**  Information on the borrowing process for financial aid, plus descriptions of direct and direct consolidation loans.

**finaid.org**  Established as a public service, this award-winning site has comprehensive information about financial aid and ways of financing your higher education.

**accessgroup.org**  The goal of Access Group is to "provide education financing to the broadest range of eligible students, positively influence education financing practices, and provide services valued by students and schools." The site has information on loan repayment, as well as an array of online services for students, families, and school administrators.

**princetonreview.com**  This info-packed site will help you search schools, discover which are best for you, apply to more than 950 schools online, and find tools for making any school affordable.

**loanconsolidation.ed.gov**  A direct consolidation loan site with borrower services, school services, and loanholder services.

OTHER STUDENT LOAN SITES

bankone.com
cfsedloans.com
tcampusdoor.com

CHAPTER

# 4

# The Potential Prison of Credit Card Debt

## *Born Free, Stay Free*

*"Magical thinking is the reality of materialism
(as well as of religion)."*

—James B. Twitchell,
*Lead Us into Temptation,* 1999

Credit cards. Keys to the Land of Acquire. You could think of it that way. Or you could see credit card debt for what it is: money that's not yours.

Let's be clear. Credit card companies are in the business of offering you their money to spend and then having you pay them for the privilege. If you pay off the full balance of your credit card bills on time each month, they'll get their money instead from the fees they charge the location where you used the card (anywhere from 3 to 4 percent of your total purchase).

I've talked at high schools where the students didn't realize that the money (more like purchasing power) credit cards gave them access to wasn't actually theirs. Many consider it free money and debt to be a part of life. Credit card companies have done a brilliant and ruthless job of getting this self-fabricated and self-serving message across.

But the reality is that the money is not yours. You are borrowing money from someone else, often at a steep cost. And as every out-of-control debtor or gambler knows, the deeper you get into the hole, the more desperate you are to get out. And the harder it gets to live your life the way you want to live it.

There are times when you need to borrow to achieve certain goals, including borrowing for college or buying your first home. And there are times when you will need to carry a fairly small credit card balance to get you by. But you should try to stay away from debt that pays for things that depreciate over time. You can make a good amount of money when you sell your home. You can make a good amount of money by landing a great career and job based on a strong education. Student loans and mortgages are there to help you get ahead in many ways. Taking on debt for a hot new suit you don't really need or a slammin' pair of retail-priced designer shoes that you can only pay for over eighteen months is nothing but debt incurred for a wasted asset.

## What Credit Card Companies Think of You (Hint: "Sucka")

Credit cards have only been around for about fifty years, but these spending enablers didn't really kick in until the 1970s— and did they ever. For example, **in 1970 the average credit**

**card holder owed $185.** Today that bloated number is around **$7,500.** In the '70s, there were approximately 20 million cards in circulation in the United States and by 2003 there were 1.3 billion—that's with a *b*—according to the Federal Reserve, for a grand total of $743 billion in revolving credit card debt.

We younger folks have taken on quite a chunk of that debt ourselves. According to CardWeb.com, credit card debt owed by young adults age eighteen to twenty-four has gone up 14 percent since 1992; the number is 55 percent for those age twenty-five to thirty-four.

But how are we to avoid this? I mean, Americans are bombarded by solicitations for credit cards and offers for credit lines and loans. PBS recently reported on a *Frontline* special that an average of six credit card offers are sent to each American household in one month—that's a total of five billion a year. This direct mail marketing, as it's called, costs credit card companies a fortune, and the response rate is absurdly low—somewhere around 1 percent.

Why are we dogged so relentlessly if there's such a dismal response rate and high costs? Well, credit card companies have become ruthlessly competitive, despite the moneymaking machines most have become. The structure of the business has created a compulsion to find new customers and to lend more and more money.

Back in the day, you had to be over eighteen and lawfully employed to get a credit card. Now my dad's dog gets a few credit card solicitations every year. (Smarty-pants Dad uses the dog's name on magazine subscriptions. The subscription database then gets sold to solicitors, so when Dad gets mail addressed to Bandit, he knows to put it directly in the shredder.)

The whole wacky idea of needing to hold a job or be an adult to get a credit card was pushed aside in the 1990s as

> "Bankers setting out to play the new credit game . . . seem to have become as blithely careless of consequences as a drunken sailor shooting craps in a Mexican whorehouse on New Year's Eve."
>
> —*Life* magazine, 1970

the market became saturated. Card company bigwigs had to scratch their chins: "Hmm. Who's left to give cards to?" The answer led the charge (*har!*) to rope in previously uncredit-worthy consumers: college students, part-timers, the unemployed, and people with bad or no credit history. Basically, the folks most in need of money, but the least likely to be able to pay it back.

And now that everyone from your 102-year-old great-grandmother to your 16-year-old sister has a credit card, how can credit card companies compete for more customers? Well, how about your favorite pop star's face on your card? How about *your* face—or any other personal photo of your choice—as is offered by the "One of a Card" Visa? The Discover Card company knows that convenience is one of the most sought-after sign-up features for credit cards, so in the late summer of 2004 it decided to allow shoppers to pay for purchases on their card with the touch of an index finger on a screen. One more payment step gone—tap the screen, and you don't even have to pull that silly card out of your wallet!

Money, costs, and debt just continue to get more and more abstract—making it all the more easy to lose control.

## Plastic Has Become the Norm

### Debit Card Downers

There's another popular and fairly new plastic-based way for banks to make money off of those who previously weren't chargers: debit cards.

Debit cards aren't a new idea, but with the ease of electronic banking and the need to reel in those last few customers who prefer to use checks and/or cash, a new piece of plastic was created for you.

They're not as bad as the scourge of credit cards—and if they're handled well, they can even be decent discipline builders. Yet debit cards still deserve a cautionary mention here, cash-based though they are, for two reasons: fees and theft.

When you use a debit card (which most banks now send you automatically as your ATM card), funds are pulled from your linked checking account right away. So how does the bank make money off you? By charging **fees** for use of the card, of course. When you buy something with your debit card—just like when you use another bank's ATM—you are charged a fee, usually $1 to $2. And because your debit card is also a Visa or MasterCard, the merchant you're buying from pays the bank a fee as well. However, if instead of using your PIN number for your purchase (making it a debit charge), you choose "credit" and sign for what you buy, you don't pay the quasi-ATM fee. (Ha!)

But the merchant is now charged a larger credit card fee, and one that is a percentage of your purchase rather than the flat fee of a dime or so when you use your PIN and "debit." Convoluted card shenanigans, but good to know.

**Theft** is another caution spot when you use debit cards. Because your debit card is usually a MasterCard or Visa, you are protected from any unauthorized charges made on your card that total more than $50. So if someone steals your credit card, no money of yours (except that $50) goes missing. But when your debit card is stolen and used, that's your hard-earned cash that's taken. Though you're covered—by bank policy, the same as with a credit card—you may not be able to get your money back into your checking account for several days while the bank processes your report. Not only could you be very broke during that time, but any checks or online payments pending can bounce and wreak some major fee havoc. This scenario happened to me several years ago, and it was a royal pain in the ass. I haven't had a debit card since.

To debit or not to debit? The answer seems to rest on how good a bill payer you are. If you can make purchases with a credit card and pay it off on time every month, my advice is to refuse debit cards. You'll save money on fees and protect your cash. But if having a credit card in your pocket makes you a spending junkie, the cash-based limits of using a debit card may help keep your spending in check.

Whatever you choose to do, though, read the fine print.

### What Type of Credit Card User Are You?

Credit card companies group their customers according to usage and bill-paying habits. What do you think they call you?

- **A deadbeat.** No, not what *we* know as a deadbeat. If you pay off your credit card bills in full and on time every month, card companies call you a deadbeat because you don't make them any money. They may not like you much, but I think you're awesome.

- **A revolver.** You may or may not pay on time, but you always carry a balance. You are credit card companies' favorite customer.
- **A rate surfer (or gamer).** You flip cards and transfer balances to get lower interest rates. You're a tad annoying to card companies, but if you just have to carry a balance—and you play it right—you may be beating them at their own game.

## SOME NAMES OF THE GAME

If you have a credit card or have ever used one, you're probably familiar with the following terms—and if not, it's time to get acquainted:

**APR**  The annual percentage rate (APR) you are charged for use of credit. More plainly, this is the percent more you'll owe and pay every year as a fee for borrowing the money. It's also referred to as the **interest rate.**

**Periodic rate**  The interest rate you're charged on your purchases or balance each month. To calculate your periodic rate, divide your APR by 12. It's also referred to as a **finance charge.**

**Fixed rate or variable rate**  If you have a **fixed** interest rate on your card, the APR will not change from month to month—*but* read your card agreement to find out how and when it could change as a penalty because you're late with payments or have gone over your limit. A **variable** rate can change monthly. If you have a variable rate—and most of us do—

keep an eye on your monthly statements to watch your rate for changes.

**Grace period** The time period—measured from the moment of purchase—during which you are not charged any interest, usually twenty-five to twenty-eight days. The practice of offering grace periods is shrinking, so make sure your card has one and confirm how long it is.

> **HINTS ON CHOOSING A CREDIT CARD**
> - Go for the lowest APR you can find, and preferably fixed.
> - Avoid annual fees.
> - Read the fine print on any other fees and potential changes in interest rate.
> - Avoid reward cards. They tend to have higher fees, and you need to charge so much to break even in rewards, it's not worth it.

**Annual fee** What you are charged each year for the privilege of using the card. It can be avoided, so please do. Other fees include: balance transfer fees, cash advance fees, special services, and over-limit charges.

**Outstanding balance** The full amount you owe on the card, including any fees.

**Finance charge** The monthly fee added to your balance, based on the monthly interest rate. It's determined by dividing your APR by 12, then multiplied by your outstanding balance.

As you can see, there are complicated costs associated with signing up for a credit card and not paying it off in full every month. Of course, in best possible worlds, not carrying a balance should be the case for everyone. Fortunately for the credit card industry, it's not.

## The Way Out

If you're currently in credit card debt and want to get out, do not despair. There is always a way.

1. **Stop charging right away.** Commit yourself to it. Make it a practice to live off a cash ration alone. Take a second job if you have to. Take only cash with you when you go out. Keep only one or two cards on lockdown at home—an American Express and/or a MasterCard or Visa. Almost all vendors accept at least one of these cards if you need to use them (in an emergency, of course).

2. **Pull together all your current credit card bills** and rank them in order of highest APR (*not* outstanding balance)— see the chart that follows. If any of your cards have APRs over 10 percent, and you have a good record of paying on time, call the customer service department and ask if the company can lower your rate. Unless you've been delinquent on payments, it usually will lower your rate. Ten minutes on the phone and you can shave off a percentage point or two and save a bunch on total interest paid and owed.

3. Once you're done with step 2, you've hopefully gotten some interest rates down. Based on these new APRs, **order your statements again,** in APR-descending order, with the highest interest rate first. With this in hand, you're ready to fill in the following chart. What you're doing here is concentrating all your debt-blasting power on the card that is charging you the highest interest rate—your most expensive loan.

4. In the meantime, **pay—on time!—all your other credit card bills** with a minimum payment only. Then, once

you've knocked out the balance on the card at the top of the list, take the *whole* amount you had been pledging to that card and apply it to the next card on the list, and so on and so on until all those suckers have been wiped out.

## Credit Card Debt Payoff Strategy

| Company | APR | Outstanding Balance | Minimum Due | Monthly Payment |
|---------|-----|---------------------|-------------|-----------------|
|         |     |                     |             |                 |
|         |     |                     |             |                 |
|         |     |                     |             |                 |
|         |     |                     |             |                 |

**Example:**

| Company | APR | Outstanding Balance | Minimum Due | Monthly Payment |
|---------|-----|---------------------|-------------|-----------------|
| Company A | 14.5% | $1,288 | $42 | $220 |
| Company B | 12.25% | $875 | $24 | $24 |
| Company C | 8.5% | $2,450 | $78 | $78 |

Watching your balance go down and crossing cards one after the other off your list will make your chest swell (with pride, that is).

And if you follow these next two edicts, you may never end up in credit card debt again. They're called **discipline** and **savvy.**

It makes sense to buy a washing machine with a credit card when you have the cash in the bank to pay for it. You'd get some serious looks if you started laying down several hundred dollars of cash at the register. And paper checks are becoming a hassle and obsolete. So we can agree that credit cards are a necessity and can be used as a handy tool for managing purchases.

But you need to do two things: Don't charge anything that you don't already have cash in the bank for. That's the "discipline" part. Then, pay your credit card bill as soon as it hits your mailbox. It's best not to let it sit there too close to the due date—this is where "savvy" comes in.

## GET SAVVY OR GET SCREWED

Credit card companies have nearly hit the ceiling of potential living customers, and credit card offers flood the streets. So the quest to make a profit continues, resting just on this side of the law.

Did you ever notice that your credit card company's return address tends to be located in Delaware, Virginia, Utah, Arizona, or South Dakota? This is because these states have few or no laws limiting how high interest rates can be on your account.

*But I pay my bills on time and I got my rates pretty low—you say—so why do I need to keep tabs on this stuff?*

Well, this would be because:

- Credit card companies can **change your interest rate** at any time and for nearly any reason, only giving you fifteen days' written notice.
- **Universal default** is now the norm. This means that if you're late on *any* loan or credit card payment, another card company with which you are in good standing can raise your interest rate and dub you a higher credit risk.

- In 1996, the Supreme Court lifted its restrictions on **late fees.** Credit card companies can charge you whatever they like as a late fee. The average late fee is now around $29—and climbing.
- Most credit card processing centers now require your payment to be received by noon on the **due date.** Anytime after that—say, 3 PM or the last mail drop at 4 PM that same day—triggers a late fee and a possible jump in your interest rate.
- Federal interest rate hikes (which APRs are based on) have raised **punitive interest rates** up to 25 to 30 percent, if you've missed payments and/or charge over a credit limit.
- According to CardWeb.com, **over-limit fees** went up 17 percent from 2001 to 2004, to an all-time-high average of $33.50.
- Again, **grace periods** have been shrinking from twenty-eight days to twenty-three—and for an increasing number of credit cards, there is no grace period at all. On these cards, the second you sign the receipt for a credit card purchase, the interest ticker starts ticking.

## CAUTION!

BALANCE TRANSFERS

*"Here's a check! Transfer your balances now!"*

We've all gotten these in the mail. But beware: Balance transfer fees can be 3 to 5 percent of the total amount you transfer (read the fine print in the agreement). And that low-APR offer may only

**TRUE BLESSINGS**

Register online with
**www.donotcall.gov** and you
won't get solicitation calls
disturbing your sleep-in
Saturdays—or any other day.
   And to stop the solicitation
junk in your mailbox and save a
few trees, call **888-50PT-OUT.**

last for three to six months.
Then it gets jacked up to a
much higher APR. Keep track!

### PRE-APPROVED OFFERS

*"You're pre-approved for this low,
low rate!"*

What reward do you get
from credit card companies
when you pay your bills on
time? Oh, just a pile of solicitations for pre-approved credit
cards in the mail and your e-mail box.

You may think, *Oh joy! I can now get a new card with 0 percent
for the first six months!* Sorry to burst your bubble (and that of
the credit card companies), but those pre-approved rates are
not guaranteed—they're teaser rates. Depending on a credit
check and review of other personal information, once you sign
up for a pre-approved card you can get any rate they deem
you worthy of, no matter what they offered you in the first
place.

### SECURED CREDIT CARDS

*"Bad credit? No credit? No problem! Get the credit you deserve!"*

Whatever you do, no matter how bad your credit history, do
your best to not sign up for a secured credit card. This is a last
resort to take if you've already declared bankruptcy.

A secured credit card requires you to open up a cash-based
bank account to act as your line of credit. The concept is no
different from a debit card, so it's wiser to get the debit card instead. Why? Because with many secured cards, fees are exorbi-

tant. The bank takes interest out of your cash deposit, then charges you monthly maintenance and processing fees, not to mention application fees on top of that. These cards also have much higher interest rates than most credit cards.

The argument for a secured credit card is that if your credit is very bad, it allows you to build up a good credit record again over time. Right, but you can open up a checking account with a bank (for little or no cost if it involves direct deposit of your paycheck) and get a debit card. If you then use it wisely, you can apply for a credit card with the same bank; it'll be more than happy to give you one with a low limit, which will get higher as you build up good credit.

## 1-900-BAD

Any credit card offer that requires you to call a 900 number (a call that should be toll-free but ends up costing anywhere from $5 to $50) is not a credit card you'd ever want. Don't do it.

### If You Have a Formal Complaint About a Credit Card Company

Mail or Fax:
Office of the Comptroller of the Currency
Customer Assistance Group
1301 McKinney Street, Suite 3450
Houston, TX 77010
Fax: 713-336-4301

#### Include a letter with the following:

- The name and address of the bank you have a complaint with.
- Your full name and the mailing address where you get your statements.
- Your daytime phone number.
- Your account number(s) with this bank.
- A detailed explanation of your complaint and what you'd like the company to do about it.
- Your signature or the signature of the primary card holder.

## THE REPORT CARD FOR GROWN-UPS

And you thought grades ended at graduation. No such luck. Your adult report card—which will be seen by dozens more people than your parents—is your **credit report,** and your final grade is your **credit score** or **FICO score.**

This rather complicated credit or FICO score (the terms are used interchangeably), which ranges between 300 and 850, was developed by the consumer credit modeler crew at Fair Isaac Corporation and can determine your whole adult financial life: from where and when you get a job (or don't) to getting a house, renting an apartment, buying a car, getting insurance, and getting a credit card.

This wildly important score is used to tell people one thing: the risk that you will not pay back a loan. It has also morphed into hinting at how likely you are to steal from the workplace, be bribed, drive recklessly and irresponsibly, or skip out on your rent.

It seems unfair. How can this one number tell anyone all these things? Well, **a credit score is based on weighing several factors:**

- Your history of paying bills on time.
- How much credit you use each month compared with the amount of credit you have available.
- The length of your credit history.
- How well you manage different kinds of debt, including credit cards, student loans, and a mortgage.
- How many other lenders (or yourself) have been looking into your records.

So if you have a low credit score (anything under 620 is frightfully bad; at or under 680 is okay; 700-plus is pretty good; and 720-plus is awesome), or you don't always pay your bills on time, or you're too deep into debt, a potential landlord or employer or insurer can extrapolate that you're a risk in other ways.

However, if your credit is overextended or if you have late payments due to a medical emergency or unforeseen catastrophe, a letter of explanation and some proactive calls can sometimes be all you need to set things right with a potential landlord, employer, or insurer. Things happen.

The keepers and creators of your credit report and credit score are these three credit reporting bureaus/agencies:

- **Equifax:**
  www.equifax.com or 800-685-1111
- **Experian:**
  www.experian.com or 888-397-3742
- **TransUnion:**
  www.transunion.com or 800-888-4213

The credit scores you get from each of these agencies are derived in slightly different ways, so you will have three separate scores. Most inquirers will go by your middle-ranking score.

*Well, crikey,* you say, *what's in these crazily important reports?* A credit report is usually composed of the following, going back **up to ten years:**

- Personal information (name, Social Security number, birth date).

To get a copy of your free credit reports—you can order all three at once, or stagger them over the year—go to: www.annualcreditreport.com or call toll-free: 877-322-8228

- Current address and previous addresses.
- Your current employer and previous employers.
- Payment history on credit cards and loans.
- Payment history of utilities and phone services.
- Any accounts that have been sent to a debt collection agency.
- When and who has made inquiries into your credit history over the past several years, along with whether you received the credit applied for or were turned down.
- Any public records, such as bankruptcies, foreclosures, or tax problems.

Now, here's some great news. Getting a copy of your own credit report from any of the credit reporting agencies used to cost from $9.99 to $19.99. But following a ruling by the Fair and Accurate Credit Transactions Act, as of September 1, 2005, you can now receive a credit report from each agency **free, once a year.**

This new free system started rolling out in December 2004 in thirteen states, swinging east across the country to the final hurrah date of 9/1/05.

It's always a good idea to see the report card that everyone else is seeing. Take advantage and once a year, every year, get a free copy of each of your three credit reports. This is not just to see where you stand, but also to review the reports for anything out of the ordinary, including potential errors or fraud.

If you spot **incorrect information** or **suspicious activity** on any of your credit reports, do the following right away:

- Inform the reporting credit agency *in writing* within sixty days of getting a copy of your report.
- Ask the credit agency to send a corrected report to anyone who has recently reviewed it.
- Keep on it—sometimes it takes a lot of persistence to set your credit report right.

SETTING THE RECORD STRAIGHT

- Closing old and/or unused credit card accounts *does not* improve your credit score.
- A long history with the same credit card or two is good for your credit score.
- Unused credit bodes well for the proportion of credit you have open compared with the portion you have in use.

A credit report is a stronghold of vital personal information, so who's allowed to see it? The only folks able to request and receive a copy of your credit report and score are:

- Banks and credit card companies.
- Other potential lenders (legitimate business organizations only).
- A potential employer (only with your permission!).
- Insurance companies.
- Government agencies that provide benefits to you.
- A potential landlord.

You can be denied credit or a rental home or insurance coverage due to a bad credit report. But if a **potential employer**

> One of the strongest positive factors on a credit report is **a major credit card in good standing.**

fails to hire you because of your credit history, the firm needs to inform you that this is the case and give you instructions on how to challenge the accuracy of the information in your report.

Credit checks by employers are becoming as popular as asking you to pee in a cup. The Society for Human Resource Management found that 35 percent of the companies surveyed checked potential employees' credit histories. Of course, it makes sense that if your job would entail handling money, transferring funds, buying or selling products, or having access to a company's financial or personnel records, you are more likely to get a credit check before getting a job offer.

## "BUT WHAT IF I'M DROWNING?"

Say you've done all you can to keep your debts in check but you were in an accident, had no health insurance, and had to put your emergency room bill on your credit card. Or you lost your job and your parents aren't able to help you out while you spend three months pounding the pavement and keyboard trying to find a comparable one.

It's not always spending sprees that send people into **unmanageable debt.** The number one reason given for bankruptcy filing is unexpected medical expenses. Bad stuff happens, and without an income that allows wiggle room, living in the red can all too easily become a reality.

If you're at a point where you can't even make your minimum

payments, psychologically it can become painful to even open your mail, but hesitating or ignoring it altogether just makes it worse. You don't have to be afraid of opening your mail. You can manage your debts on terms you have some say in and get yourself back on your financial feet.

**Stay Away** from solicitations or claims such as:

"We can erase bad credit—guaranteed!"

"Credit problems? No problem!"

These are most likely disguised bankruptcies.

**Option 1.** Get those bills in order and **contact your creditors** as soon as possible—before they have to contact you. Offering a preemptive strike works highly in your favor. Let them know your situation and your willingness to work things out. Try to work out a modified payment plan that you can afford.

**Option 2.** Contact the **Consumer Credit Counseling Service.** Legitimate credit counseling services are non-profit organizations that are either free or charge minimal fees for working with you and your creditors to establish a manageable debt repayment plan. Legitimate credit counseling agencies are affiliated with the National Foundation for Credit Counseling or the Association of Independent Consumer Credit Counseling Agencies.

And stay away from any supposed credit counseling agency that:

- Charges you a high upfront fee.
- Asks for personal information without first providing free information about its services in writing.

Before you agree to anything, make sure to check out any credit counseling agency with the **Better Business Bureau** and your state attorney general's office.

In most instances—except for only the most dire—you can successfully manage your credit situation on your own (see option 1) and not spend any additional money on getting your debts in order.

But should you find yourself in a bad debt situation and you're getting calls from creditors and debt collection agencies, first run to option 1. And know that there is a **Fair Debt Collection Practices Act** that protects you from being abused by debt collectors. They are *not* allowed to:

- Require you to take their calls.
- Use profanity.
- Threaten to send you to jail.
- Misstate the amount you owe.
- Tell you that they are going to repossess property (unless they have firm plans to do so).
- Verbally threaten or abuse you.
- Call you before 8 AM or after 9 PM.

Don't let someone call you up and threaten to take your futon away. Tell the caller you know your rights under this act.

## Last Resort

Please don't do this. I am hard-pressed even to give you any information about it lest you think it's a viable option. But you're liable to hear it from someone less informed, so better you read about it here: **bankruptcy.**

Bankruptcy is serious business. It's heartbreakingly serious, and a horrible ordeal to go through. There is no simple way to get rid of your debts without incurring severe and irreparable damage to your financial future—no matter what some infomercial says. If you declare bankruptcy, you may be unable to find a new home for the next seven to ten years because you won't be wanted as a tenant. You probably won't be able to get phone service, credit cards, or possibly utilities. Not to mention how it looks to a potential employer.

Bankruptcy is a huge cop-out sign to most—no matter what happened to get you there.

*But*—if you've talked to all your creditors, contacted and tried to work with a credit counseling service, and either refinanced your home or car, or taken out a home equity loan, and bankruptcy is all you have left (short of fleeing to a tropical island), you have two bankruptcy choices:

- **Chapter 13.** In bankruptcy court, you receive a court-approved debt repayment plan that allows you to pay off a designated amount over three to five years. This allows you to keep your property and/or car.
- **Chapter 7.** This is full-blown, straight-up bankruptcy where all your assets are liquidated by the court. You'll be able to keep maybe a car so you can get to a job, and some basic household items.

Not as bad as old-fashioned debtor's prison, but horrifying nonetheless.

## INVASION OF THE ID SNATCHERS

There is one more bogeyman in this land of plastic and online shopping. Thieves no longer have to rob your wallet. They can just hack into your accounts online, scam you on the phone, or sort through your mail or garbage.

Identity theft is the **number one** consumer complaint in the country. The convenience of credit cards, electronic banking, and shopping online has made it easier for ID thieves to steal in stealth. But shopping and banking online is actually very safe and secure—it's only now that instead of just holding on tight to your wallet or purse, you have to hold tight to your information.

The responsibility to be smart about our personal information falls more and more on us as the web becomes more and more a breeding ground for scammers. New medium, new tactics.

But first a word of caution about **paper checks:** When you order your checks from your bank, don't have anything printed on them but your name. No address. No phone. Otherwise anyone who's able to intercept one of your checks will have your personal data and also your bank information, including your account number. To make things worse, the vendor may request your driver's license number. A thief would then be 98 percent of the way to opening a credit card in your name.

Too many people see paper checks as they pass along the system—so guard your information and give the minimum needed to pay bills or make a purchase.

> Consumers between 25 and 44 are the most likely to be victims of fraud.
>
> —Federal Trade Commission Consumer Fraud Survey, 2004

Back to plastic. One of the best ways to keep a preemptive eye on your information is to monitor your credit reports for any newly opened accounts

> **Shred your paper garbage.** Don't let anyone get their hands on a pre-approved credit offer!

or suspicious activity. If you catch anything, call the credit bureau right away and follow the procedures to get the account closed or frozen. If someone is stealing from you, make sure to follow up with a police report. Might as well have someone try to catch the sucker and prevent him or her from doing it to someone else—or you, again.

Your credit report will also show you if anyone has been making an inquiry into a report—for example, another credit card company looking to open an account with you. If you didn't ask for this, call the company listed and ask why they made the inquiry. You can stop the potential thief right there.

If you're still getting solicitation calls at home or online, don't give out any personal information. If it's a legitimate bank or card company, ask them to send you information by mail. Then you can check them out to make sure they're legit. If you're already registered with **www.donotcall.gov,** also call **888-567-8687** to get the three credit bureaus not to sell or share your information with solicitors.

This personal information I speak of—and which should only be stored in your head or a safe-deposit box—includes:

- Your mother's maiden name.
- Your PIN(s).
- Your Social Security number.

Guard your credit cards and their numbers, too.

Shopping online (smartly!) with a credit card (that you pay off in full and on time every month, ahem) is one of the great conveniences of modern life. Come holidays and birthdays, it's my savior.

But there are a few safety measures to use when you're shopping online to protect your identity, credit cards, and credit report:

- Shop and bank at sites with an **https** URL—the s means that it's secure.
- **Decline** saving your credit card info at the site where you shop. Sometimes with large vendors, you can't help it, but if given the option, opt out.
- Don't open any **attachments** from senders you don't know—it could contain a worm used to gain access to personal information on your computer.
- Designate one credit card as **your online card.** In this way, if someone gets ahold of it, you can cancel the card and still have one more at home for offline purchasing.
- And of course, make any **passwords** or **PINs** you use online as difficult as possible. No birthdays or mother's maiden name here—or worse, 12345! Think back to something quirky and memorable, like your homeroom number senior year in high school or the name of your first goldfish.

And here's a big new one that you've probably heard about, sure to become the biggest potential ID theft scam, and so special that it gets its own made-up name: **phishing.** The bad guys send e-mails disguised as being from a legit business and "fish" (or "phish") for your personal information. They figure if they send out enough e-mails, someone will bite.

> Look out for any mysterious magazine subscriptions that appear on your credit card bill for magazines you never ordered. Get them canceled and taken off your bill. **This is fraud.**

So don't give *any* personal information or passwords/PIN(s) in response to any e-mail request. Many ID thieves build fairly sophisticated e-mail sites with names that sound like legit vendors. If you're concerned and suspicious (which you should automatically be if they ask for any personal information), go to the real vendor's web site and report it to their customer service.

In mid-2004, phishing scam reports had gone up several thousand percent in less than a year. And according to the Anti-Phishing Working Group (APWG), as many as 3 to 5 percent of folks are falling for the hook. Remember, phishers are sophisticated and slick—but no vendor or legitimate bank would ask you to verify personal information over the web, especially unsolicited.

And please don't click on any links in the e-mail. It will only take you deeper.

Lastly, nope, you don't need credit card insurance to cover you if your card or card information is stolen and used. This is another ploy to get money out of you. The laws of the Federal Trade Commission cover all credit card holders from theft and fraudulent charges after the first $50.

Happy (smart) charging.

## Web Links

**ftc.gov**  The site of the Federal Trade Commission, with consumer and business information on credit, identity theft, and other consumer topics.

**equifax.com**  One of the big-three credit bureaus. You can get your credit score and reports here, as well as info on managing your credit and protecting yourself against theft.

**idtheftcenter.org**  The Identity Theft Resource Center offers help for victims of identity theft, and prevention information for others.

**consumer.gov**  Consumer research information from government. There's a special section on identity theft, with tips on what to do if you think your identity has been stolen.

**bankrate.com**  A great site for tools and information on credit cards, loans, and general banking info. Also debt payoff and various interest rate calculators.

**cardweb.com**  The U.S. Payment Card Information Network provides info on credit cards, debit cards, ATM cards, phone cards, and other payment cards.

**dmaconsumers.org**  This is the site of the Direct Marketing Association—the trade association of those businesses that call you to sign up for credit cards. It offers tips and advice about shopping and your rights as a consumer.

**myfico.com**  The home page of the folks who started credit scores. You'll find credit information and personal credit tools, a way to get your scores and reports, debt calculators, and info on protecting your credit.

**download.com** This site enables you to "try-before-you-buy" certain software. You'll also find different personal finance software, spreadsheet software, and other business- and personal-finance-related downloads.

**donotcall.gov** Register with these folks! This is the site where you can sign up to stop solicitation calls from credit card companies and other telemarketing businesses.

**experian.com** Another of the three leading credit bureaus, Experian's site lets you get your credit score and report, and helps you to understand and manage your credit information.

**transunion.com** The final big-three credit bureau site, Trans-Union, offers products and services on financial security, credit reports and scores, and tips on preventing fraud.

**annualcreditreport.com** Go here *before* you visit any of the big-three credit bureau sites to get your annual free credit report online.

CHAPTER
# 5

# To Rent, Perchance to Buy

*Managing Your Casa*

Living on your own is probably something we've all looked forward to since our parents set up curfews and started snooping in our rooms. Elsewhere, the norm is for a young adult to live at home until marriage. Not so in the U.S. of A. Many of us jumped at the chance to be on our own at eighteen or twenty-one, or as soon as fiscally possible. Independence is the American way.

However, due to the ever-mounting expenses of living independently, combined with student loans and credit card debt—not to mention paltry starting salaries—more and more young adults are choosing to live at home with parents or other family until late into their twenties. And who can blame them? Free or very low rent, food, and maybe they're lucky enough to have their laundry done, too.

This chapter is for when you do make that big move out on your own (or with a partner). And even later, when you decide to take the plunge and purchase your first home. Laws may change state by state, but the basics of rental units and home purchasing remain pretty much the same. And since I've been through it all, I'll boil it down for you so it seems a tad less daunting.

## WHERE SHOULD I LIVE?

Are you planning on staying in your hometown? Or are you following a job to a new city or state? Is there a spot that you've just been aching to check out because you've dreamed of warmer climes and better food all your life?

If you're looking to move and want to check out some basic demographics and costs of living for different areas in the United States, there are some great spots online. **Yahoo! Real Estate** lists comprehensive info on specific neighborhoods across the country. **CNNMoney.com** has an annual Best Places to Live list that's fairly subjective, but has good cultural and entertainment information for various hot real estate markets. These sites also give you an idea of the local employment climate. Finding out what the **job market** is like in a city or county is very important not only for your employment prospects, but also when it comes to crime, local businesses and restaurants, and rental or home-buying rates.

Go online to check out local newspapers to get an insider's idea of the flavor and tone of the locale. You can also read about certain parts of town that you should be wary of or read up on community developments.

Basically, when it comes to choosing a spot to live, many

**WHEN LOOKING FOR A SPOT TO LIVE, ASK:**

- How far is the nearest public transportation?—or, is it safe where I have to park my car?
- Where's the nearest hospital and police precinct?
- Is there a school nearby where kids may be very noisy?
- What would be my commute?
- Any heavy construction nearby?
- Is it well lit at night?

times your level of satisfaction with your choice has most to do with how much detective work you do beforehand. And don't just stick to the computer screen—ask friends, family, and acquaintances about where you're interested in setting up shop. You'd be surprised at how small the world is. All of a sudden you find out that your long-lost godmother lives in Austin and has the inside scoop on an apartment downtown that will be vacant in a couple of months. Cast your investigation net wide and far and you'll be miles ahead when you make your move.

If you're making the move to a major city but will be on a tight budget, don't rule out the local ethnic enclaves where rent and housing prices will be cheaper, and your neighbors may be more inclined to look after you and be neighborly. You'll also eat better on $5 than ever before. If you're worried about feeling out of place, you may be surprised to find out that sprinkled around you are fellow former students, young teachers, and artists.

Just make sure that your transportation is safe and that you feel safe.

## RENTING

If you're planning on moving again in a year or two or are not sure if your job is stable yet and you're living tight, renting is probably the way to go.

Strangely, in many U.S. cities right now, the real estate market is such that renting is actually a good thing to do rather than the "throwaway" money that most people think it is. Radically enough, the housing market is on a huge upswing; thousands of former renters have become buyers in the past couple of years. I'll get into the whole interest rate and cheap mortgages deal in a bit, but essentially, if the housing market continues to surge ahead, there is now and will continue to be a shortage of renters for the markets that need them.

As a result, landlords have been throwing incentives at potential renters—one month free, or a newly installed washer/dryer, or even much cheaper rent—to woo the fewer and fewer available renters. In early 2004, *Business 2.0* magazine reported that the rental apartment market in 2003 had the highest vacancy rate in fifteen years. It also reported in December 2004 that rents in many locales have been knocked back to the levels of ten years ago and that potential renters now have tremendous bargaining power. So, all things continuing as such, cheap rent can be found.

### A-HUNTING WE WILL GO

There are many ways to go hunting for a rental; it mostly depends on your local housing market. But no matter where you are, do your best to avoid paying a Realtor or management fee. With the rental market greeting you, future renter, with wide-open arms, you can avoid paying a real estate agent a fee or another company a finder's fee by:

- Visiting local college and university **campuses** to look for listings posted on communal bulletin boards or in campus newspapers.
- Going online to your local **Craigslist.com** to find apartments for rent or to post your own "Wanted" listing.
- Sending an **e-mail** to friends and family letting them know where you're looking and asking them to spread the word for you.
- Walking or slowly driving around **potential neighborhood(s)** and looking for FOR RENT signs or the contact information of the management company listed on the buildings you're interested in. Make sure to follow up quickly with what you find.

So you've seen a fabulous pad and just know in your gut it's the one for you. But first, before you fall completely in lust and hand over a check, make sure you:

- Flush **toilets** and run all the faucets (kitchen and bathrooms) to check for **water pressure.**
- Make sure all **appliances** work (refrigerator, stove, thermostats).
- Look for electrical **outlets** and telephone **jacks.**
- Check to see if you'll need new and better **locks** on the doors and windows and if the landlord will pay for any **safety** improvements.

- Visit during a time of day when you're more likely to be at home (say, early mornings and evenings) so you can check the **noise** levels inside and the neighborhood **people traffic.**

No place will be absolutely perfect, but if these basics hold up to your satisfaction and the price is right, it may be time to set up that lease.

### RENTAL AGREEMENTS AND LEASES

This is definitely a case where you need to read the fine print. Make sure to peruse your rental agreement or lease **line by line** and bring up any concerns or disagreements before you sign. And if the lease period seems too long or

> **WHEN YOU MOVE, INFORM:**
> - credit card companies
> - student loans
> - bank
> - employer
> - utilities
> - subscriptions
> - former landlord
> - friends and family
>
> The postal service has a great mail-forwarding page on its web site (**moversguide.usps .com**), but it's not guaranteed that your mail will find you. You don't want to miss any credit card or loan payments because you never got the bill—**they don't take that as an excuse.**

> **Protect yourself:**
> Always get a rental agreement in writing.

you're not sure how long you're going to stay put, this is the time to see if you can go month to month, rather than commit to a year or two.

## A rental lease should include the following:

- The amount of monthly rent due and when and how the amount can be raised if it's not fixed for the full term of the lease.

- How long you're agreeing to live there.
- How and where your security deposit will end up and if it will be used to pay for damages you make to the apartment (not legal in some states) while you're there, or if it's for rental coverage only.
- Any potential extra charges such as for use of a communal washer/dryer or increased utility costs during a certain particular season.
- How many people can occupy the space.
- If you're allowed a pet and/or any pet restrictions.
- Rules for subletting (renting your place out to a third party).

Rent is usually due the first of the month, but it can be on any date the landlord decides. Remember, though, that with rent there are no grace periods—if you're late by one day, your lease can become void and the landlord can either charge a late fee or make you leave.

The expensive part of renting (if you're not paying a fee) is the security deposit. Landlords have a right to ask for a month or two of rent up front in addition to your first month's rent payment. The **security deposit** protects the landlord in case you decide to skip out or cause damage. There are state limits on how much of a security deposit landlords can ask for, and they are required to hold the deposit in a bank account.

> **DC, CA, MD, NJ, & NY**
> . . . have rent-control laws limiting the amount a landlord can charge in rent and the amount this can increase from year to year or lease to lease.

If all goes well, your security deposit must be sent back to you (with interest, if there is any) within **fourteen to thirty days after you move out.**

If the landlord decides to take money out of your security deposit for any damages, he or she is required to list and inform you in writing what the exact damages were and the cost of repair and subsequent deduction.

Though you are technically on your landlord's property, you do have **privacy rights** that should be followed. Again, there are state-to-state differences here, but overall most landlords are allowed to enter the property only:

- In an emergency.
- To make major repairs.
- To show the place to prospective new tenants or buyers.

Most landlords can also enter your apartment if you've been gone for an extended period of time (usually more than a week) to make sure all's well.

In any of these instances or if you need an exterminator, for example, landlords should give you **twenty-four hours' notice.**

Speaking of repairs, some landlords can be negligent. If you have any major repairs that are not being taken care of—such as no hot water or working toilet, or severe leaks—you have **rights as a tenant** as well. If your landlord is negligent, in most states you can:

- Pay less rent until the repair is made.
- Withhold rent until the repair is made.
- Hire someone on your own to make the repairs and deduct the cost from your rent.
- Leave before your lease is up.

Remember to check your local laws in such cases.

Of course when vacating a rental, there is going to be regular wear and tear. But anything beyond that—such as cigarette burns, broken tiles, excessive stains, and wall damage—may mean the landlord can charge you for any work that needs to be done.

If you need to break a rental lease, the best thing you can do is be very **nice** and **respectful** about it. Don't just give as much notice to your landlord as possible, but offer to find a new tenant as well. Most landlords will be fine with this, but if not, you may need to pay all the remaining rent. It's rare, though, that a landlord would be such a curmudgeon as to make you do this, and many states actually require the landlord to release you from your lease if there is good cause—job transfer, marriage, family emergency.

### ROOMIES

You've got a great job in a city you've always wanted to live in but darn it, you just can't afford to live alone. Roommates can be a nightmare—there is no doubt about that—but you may have no choice. You might also really want to live with your best friend or someone else to save money, or feel safe, or have fun.

My biggest recommendation is that you sign a **joint lease.** In this way, you're both (or all) responsible for the rent and the apartment or home should one of the roomies decide to skip town. The onus, though, is equally on you—each roommate shares full legal responsibility. This means that the full rent is due even if one of you decides not to pay. And it's perfectly legal for your landlord to demand a single check every month from the group (rather than processing several checks for different amounts).

Here's the scary thing—no matter how loud, nasty, or dirty your roommate is, only the landlord can legally evict someone whose name is on the lease. If the roommate won't leave, but you're miserable, it's up to you to find a new pad.

When you move in with a roommate—especially a stranger—you should set up a **roommate agreement** *pronto* and in writing. Why not set the standards early and avoid future fiascos? Plus, a roommate agreement shows you mean business at the get-go. A good roommate agreement should include:

- Who pays the **rent** each month and how much each roommate owes.
- Who pays which **utilities** (try parceling out the utilities among roommates so no one person is responsible for all).
- Any rules about overnight **visitors** and **noise** (especially if you or a roommate works from home or is a student).
- What rules there are for sharing **food,** or if each roommate is responsible for his or her own.
- The **cleaning** schedule and responsibilities.
- The procedures if one or more roommates decide to move out before the lease is up—how much **notice** is required and who will find the next tenant.

## TIME TO BUY?

So you got a great promotion. You love your new city or town and you've decided to stick around. Is it time to push aside the fiddling of rentals and buy your next home?

Yes, there is a strange and almost nationwide housing situation now in which the rental and housing market is a tad unbalanced. But there really is something satisfying, not to mention financially savvy, in buying a home. It's an investment that rarely *fails* to pay off if you stay put for at least four to five years.

According to *Money* magazine in 2003, over the past thirty years home prices in the United States overall have never declined from one year to the next. Nationwide, housing prices have risen on average a total of 38 percent from 1997 to 2002. According to the National Association of Realtors, **the average home value increases 6 percent a year.**

Now, real estate is a local phenomenon, meaning that the level that home prices go up or remain stagnant depends on the local economy and job market. There are many stories of major cities and towns where a local industry decides to move overseas to find cheaper labor and property values take a plunge. However, it's amazing how many of these formerly depressed places are geared for an upswing or are already on their way. What goes down usually comes back up, eventually.

Between heavy immigration and our increasingly information-based economy, it looks like the housing market will continue to rise in major cities and suburbs. Of course, when it comes to home as an investment—not just a roof over your head—we all wish we could see the returns of Las Vegas, where home values (according to CNNMoney.com) went up 53.7 percent from 2003 to 2004. Heck, I'd settle for the OC (Orange County, California) at a rise of 26 percent that year, or even Tucson, Arizona, at a healthy 12.6 percent. As the saying goes: **Location, location, location.**

Ask any homeowner, though: Buying and taking care of a home is rarely a piece of cake. Remember that it's a big financial and personal step with a sharp jump in responsibility and expenses. There's no landlord to fix that leaky toilet, or patch holes in the wall, or fix that broken lock. **It's all you.** You own it, and it's up to you to fix the problems that will notoriously creep up on a new homeowner—especially a first-timer. But if you do your homework and don't let emotion do the ruling, you'll avoid any potential money pits and feel a well-earned, awesome pride in getting the deal done.

### LET'S BUY
**Before you decide to buy a home, ask yourself these questions:**

- Am I staying put for at least three or four years?
- Is there any potential of getting a job transfer?
- Can I count on my income to stay constant or get better?
- Do I have enough cash on hand for upfront costs, plus a cushion for just-in-cases as well?

If you answered yes to all of the above *except* the second question, you're probably all set to get your house hunting started.

### HUNTING, TAKE TWO
Looking for a home to buy is a tad more complicated than looking for a rental. It's important to make sure not only that the structure is in good condition and that you feel secure in the locale, but also that you know what the property taxes are and how good or bad the **school district** is. The latter is important whether you have children or not: A good school district bodes

> Bring a digital or Polaroid **camera** and a **notebook** with you on your house hunt.

well for a future sale. It's a great advantage for any potential buyer.

**Property taxes** can be a huge annual cost on top of your mortgage, and they rise with the rising value of your property. The amount of property tax on a home can give you an idea of the worth of the location vs. another home with a similar asking price across town. You can ask the Realtor about the property tax on the house you are interested in or look it up in town records.

To be well prepared for your house hunt, keep these several points in mind:

- **Clean up your credit report.** Before you hit the pavement, order the annual free copies of your credit report from the three credit bureaus and look for anything out of the ordinary that needs to be fixed or for any way you can bring up your score.

- **Calculators.** There are great mortgage calculators on the web (I list some later in this chapter). Use them to get an idea of how much house you can afford—but always shoot a bit lower, rather than higher, than

> **MULTIPLE-UNIT LINGO:**
>
> **Co-op (cooperative)**
> A residence where each owner is a shareholder in the building. Owners are partners, not outright property owners. The co-op board has control over who can buy into the building or not.
>
> **Condo (condominium)***
> Each owner is an outright owner of each unit. Common charges are levied for the maintenance of shared areas.
> *Preferred over co-ops.*

what you're quoted. The general rule is, you can probably afford a home with a purchase price **two and a half times** your annual salary. For example, if you earn $50,000, you can fairly easily afford a mortgage of $125,000. This may seem conservative, but part of the reason people get so mired in debt is **overextension.** Let's say you get a mortgage that's closer to three times your salary or a bit more. And you lose your job. Or not even that dramatic: You are so stretched with your mortgage payments, property taxes, home repairs, utility bills—not to mention credit card or student loan debt and car payments and costs—that you have no room to save or pay off your debts. That's why it's better to calculate in some wiggle room. Stick to two and a half.

- **Compare.** Also check online (see **domania.com**) as to what comparable homes are going for in the same general location or neighborhood so you know what a fair price is and approximately how much leeway you have to bid below (or above) the asking price.

## MORTGAGES

Maybe .01 percent of home buyers actually pay the full amount for a new home in cash. When us regular folks purchase a home, we're taking out a loan from a bank or other lender for most of the price. Our loan or mortgage payments give us more and more ownership of our home as time goes by (that's called **equity**). Our slice of the home pie gets bigger and bigger as the mortgage gets paid off, and so does our net worth.

When it comes to mortgages, the most important number is your **interest rate.** As with credit cards (but obviously on a much bigger scale, I hope), you're charged interest for borrowing the money you need to pay for your home. There are many factors that determine the interest rate on your mortgage, and most are within your control.

What you're not in charge of is the basic interest rate set by the Federal Reserve that determines the basis of mortgage rates. Right now, mortgage rates are at a forty-year low because the Fed's interest rate is at a historical low. If the Fed decides to bring rates up, mortgage rates go up.

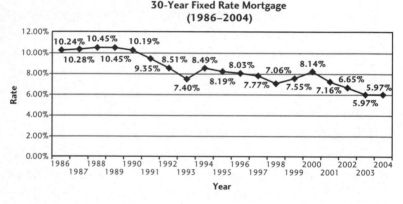

**30-Year Fixed Rate Mortgage
(1986–2004)**

How much house you can afford depends on the funds you have available to pay your mortgage and other housing costs each month. The interest rate that you get on your mortgage can make $100 or so difference in your monthly payment.

There are many mortgage calculators online that have you plug in your salary and other info to show you how much of a mortgage you can afford to take on. But be cautious—some sites are come-ons from a bank or lender trying to sign you up for a mortgage that's too big for you to handle. Instead, go to sites such as money.com or bankrate.com that are fairly conservative and not selling anything.

> **MORTGAGE CALCULATORS**
> goodmortgage.com
> bankrate.com
> mortgage-calculator.us.com

A basic rule to follow is that your total monthly home costs (including mortgage payment, property taxes, and home insurance) should not exceed **28 percent** of your gross monthly income (that's your monthly pay before taxes).

> **"I can afford about $1,500 a month"**
>
> That's a mortgage of:
> $_____
> at _____%
> **or** $_____
> at _____%

If you're a **first-time home buyer,** this is a time to be conservative. One reason there are so many young adult bankruptcies lately is that many first-timers took out loans that were too big. All it takes is one financial road bump—say, a job loss, an expensive medical emergency, or crazy credit card bills—and a mortgage payment or two can't be made. Better to be safe—don't overextend yourself, keep financial breathing and saving room—than sorry.

Seemingly backward, you'll probably be **shopping for a mortgage** before you start shopping for a home. Getting set up with a loan makes you much more attractive to a potential seller and just may push you to the front of the line, if there is one.

> The number of home buyers under the age of 25 **doubled** from 1992 to 2002.
> —*Money,* 2003

It's simple to get **pre-qualified** for a mortgage. This is when a potential lender lets you know how much it would be willing to lend you for a mortgage based on your financial information. However, the lender hasn't made any commitment to you at this point.

What you'd be better off doing is getting **pre-approved.** Here, the lender takes all your information, checks your credit record and history, and makes you a firm loan offer at a certain interest rate that is good for a limited period of time (usually thirty to sixty days).

Mortgage shopping can get *very* interesting. It's like being in the toothpaste aisle for the first time in your life, having to choose among 120 kinds of toothpaste. "Oh, what about this one?" "Do I need tartar control more, or whitening?"

If you're a first-timer, though, there is one mortgage choice question we can bypass, and that's how long your mortgage will be. Mortgages come in **thirty-year, twenty-year,** and **fifteen-year** flavors. Now, considering that the term of your student loan is usually ten to twelve years, imagine affording a loan ten times as big in a term of fifteen or twenty years. Probably not, eh? Yeah, me neither. We're going to go with a **thirty-year mortgage,** thanks.

> To APPLY FOR A MORTGAGE, PULL THESE THINGS TOGETHER:
> - **pay stubs** for the past month
> - Most recent **bank account** statements
> - Most recent **credit card** statements
> - Last two **tax returns** and W-2 and 1099 forms
> - Most recent documents/bill/ **paybook** for your car and/or student loan(s)
> - Any **brokerage** account statements for the past month
> - Most recent **IRA** or **401(k)** statements

After your mortgage time frame is set, there are three basic types of mortgages available, based on interest rates and payment practices. It can seem overwhelming, but if you ask the right questions, you can quickly find out which is right for you:

### FIXED

This mortgage has an interest rate that is locked in for the full life of the loan. Ask yourself:

- Do I plan on staying put for more than five years?
- Are interest rates really low right now?

If you answered yes to both of these questions, this is the mortgage for you.

### ARM (ADJUSTABLE-RATE MORTGAGE)

A fairly new and very popular choice recently, an ARM is a mortgage where the interest rate either fluctuates month to month or is fixed for an initially agreed-on period of time, then adjusts monthly. A **5/1 ARM** gives you five years of a fixed interest rate; then the rate changes from month to month. **7/1s** and **3/1s** are also available. Note that the more risk you assume, the lower your interest rate on an ARM. So a 3/1 ARM will have a lower interest rate than a 5/1 or 7/1.

ARMs have tangibly lower interest rates than fixed mortgages, but if interest rates go up, your monthly mortgage can run up drastically and be a major strain on your budget. Ask yourself:

- Do I plan on moving in less than five years?
- Are interest rates fairly high right now?

**Should I use a real estate agent or broker to find a home?**

If you're moving to a new city or town, the answer is definitely **yes.**

You need someone on your home-buying team who knows the locale and the local businesses.

A yes to both questions probably means an ARM is for you. The lower interest rate can save you money in the short term, especially if you're planning on moving soon.

### INTEREST-ONLY MORTGAGE

An interest-only mortgage has you pay only the interest on your loan for a set period (say, five, seven, or fifteen years); then principal payments (payments that actually go toward the amount you borrowed) kick in. You can end up with a substantially lower monthly mortgage payment at first (and therefore can afford a bigger mortgage), but you won't be building equity in your home (unless you're disciplined enough to make payments on the principal anyway). When the principal due kicks in, it may hurt—a lot.

- Am I sure that I'm going to have a big jump in income or salary in a couple of years?
- Am I planning on moving within three to five years?

| $200,000 30-YEAR FIXED MORTGAGE | |
|---|---|
| Interest Rate | Monthly Payment |
| Fixed @ **6%** | $1,199.10 |
| ARM @ **4.2%**\* | $978.03 |
| ARM @ **6.8%**\* | $1,303.85 |
| Interest-only @ **4%** | $666.66 |

*\*ARM rates jumped this much between 1904 and 1995.*
—*Money*, 2003

Two yesses on this one and an interest-only mortgage may be for you.

I'm fairly conservative when it comes to taking on the financial responsibility of a big mortgage, so when I bought my first home with the hubby, I chose to follow the **7/7 rule:**

- Do we plan on staying put for 7 years or more?
- Are interest rates on a fixed mortgage at or below 7 percent?

Our answers to both questions were yes, so we went with a fixed-rate mortgage. Shoot, I remember when my dad was paying almost 16 percent interest on our family mortgage. Anything at or below 7 percent is a historical booty.

Now, you could make that a 6/6 rule, but basically a fixed mortgage protects you from unpredictable housing costs and keeps your rate low even if rates later rise. An adjustable-rate mortgage is best if fixed rates are high and you're planning on moving in a couple of years.

## POINTS

If interest rates are high and you're planning on keeping your home for several years, you may want to do a funky thing and pay points.

Here is where lenders allow you to pay some interest up front (**1 point = 1 percent interest**) so you can land a lower interest rate on the loan. Let's say you agree to being charged a point. You'll pay 1 percent of your mortgage (for a $200,000 mortgage, that would be $2,000) at closing, and your interest rate on the loan would go from 8 to 7 percent.

Paying so much interest up front is an advantage only if you stay put and

| 10 YEARS—A $200,000 MORTGAGE AT: | |
| --- | --- |
| 8%→**$89,538.08** total interest paid | |
| 7%→**$77,424.68** total interest paid | |

keep the mortgage for several years. That extra percentage point adds up over the life of the loan to much more than what you paid up front for the point.

## HOME SHOPPING

Now that you know what you're looking for in a mortgage, it's time to shop. Back in the day, mortgage shopping meant picking up the phone and calling banks one by one or, worse, going door to door looking for the best deal from lenders.

> **BAIT-AND-SWITCH**
> Stay away from a lender or broker that offers you a great rate then ups it as the deal gets closer. If this happens, fight to get it back to what was initially offered. If they still don't give you the originally quoted rate, **walk away.**

Thankfully, most lenders are online now, so you won't need to leave your desk until you decide whom you're going with. The problem with so much convenience is that the number of choices is a tad overwhelming—and it's tough to gauge who's on the up-and-up.

Start with a site such as **nationalmortgage.com**—these folks will give you a good group of legit lenders and have each get back to you with their offer. And to find out where interest rates on various types of loans are in general right now, go to bankrate.com to see what lenders are offering.

> **Myfico.com** allows you to see mortgage rates by credit scores.

So if it's all at our fingertips, why do we keep hearing about **mortgage brokers**? Mortgage brokers do the mortgage shopping for you. They take all your information, contact lenders, and present you with the best rate. However, some mortgage brokers get paid by tacking on a percentage fee to your interest rate. So if they get you a rate of 6.5 percent, you can assume that it would be a bit lower if you'd shopped on your own. Some are paid instead by a flat processing fee. Mortgage brokers are definitely worth it if you're in a time crunch, because they have established relationships with many lenders and know not only from whom to get the best deal, but also how to get preferred rates—they bring these lenders new customers.

> ### Should I Prepay the Principal on my Mortgage?
>
> - Your mortgage is probably the **least expensive** (though it's the biggest) debt you have—plus, you get tax breaks.
> - Don't enroll in a prepay agreement with a lender—they charge **fees.**
> - **If your other debts are taken care of** and you want to make higher payments on your home, simply add what you can to your usual mortgage payment, marking off that the extra funds are to go toward principal—it's free!

I didn't have a lot of time to mortgage-shop, so I used a mortgage broker and held firm to make sure he got us the lowest rate we could get and didn't pull a bait-and-switch, sticking us with a higher rate than promised come purchasing time.

## Down Payments and Piggybacks

The number one reason why most renters can't and don't become buyers is because they don't have the cash for a down payment. There is no doubt that coming up with 20 percent of

$180,000 is a kicker (that'd be $36,000 . . . cash). And traditionally, no down payment of 20 percent (or more), no house.

Well, there is this thing called **PMI** (private mortgage insurance) that is thankfully becoming a practice of the past. Basically, if you couldn't come up with the full 20 percent down payment, a lender would charge you about .5 percent of your total loan amount—adding it to your mortgage payments—as a kind of insurance should you not be able to handle your mortgage.

But instead of having to pay PMI, many lenders, and especially the government, have created several ways that first-time home buyers with good credit can buy a home with much less than a 20 percent down payment—and sometimes with no down payment at all.

First off, the **Federal Housing Administration** has great low rates and low down payment requirements for mortgages up to around $280,000. Check out its programs at hud.gov. **Fannie Mae Flex mortgages** are also a great deal (see FannieMae.com or FreddieMac.com). You can borrow around $300,000 with very little or no down payment. (These are tied to the government, so you know it's legit.) The Flex 100 offers full mortgage financing—no down payment—and the Flex 97 requires only a 3 percent down payment.

Another way to bypass paying PMI is to take out an **80/20 mortgage.** If you have good credit, an 80/20 mortgage allows you to take out a second mortgage for the 20 percent down payment, though it will be at a higher interest rate than your bigger mortgage. It's a bit more expensive but it's a better deal than paying PMI, which gives you no equity or return on your money.

Another option is to take out a **piggyback loan.** You start by getting your initial mortgage of 80 percent of the purchase price, and then pay for 10 to 15 percent of the rest of the price (traditionally part of your down payment) with a piggybacked home equity loan or home equity line of credit (HELOC).

A **home equity loan** is a lump-sum, fixed-rate loan separate from your mortgage, usually with a ten- to twelve-year term. A **HELOC** is also a separate loan but has a flexible interest rate that can adjust from month to month. Right now, each of these has an interest rate even lower than your mortgage, since the rates on these loans are tied to the Federal Reserve prime rate.

> **Don't take out a home equity loan to pay credit card bills (unless the alternative is bankruptcy).**
>
> If you default on a home equity loan, *your home is at stake.*

There won't be any surprises with a home equity loan—the rate is fixed for the life of the loan—but if you end up with a HELOC, you may want to take any extra funds and pay it off more quickly than required. If interest rates start climbing, a HELOC can quickly become the most expensive debt you own.

> **First-time home buyers can use the following for a down payment without any penalties:**
>
> - An IRA or 401 (k) (but you will have to pay taxes)
> - A cash gift up to $11,000 from each parent

## CLOSING COSTS: THEY'RE A DOOZY

Oh, but there is no buying a home without forking over some cash—80/20s and Flex 100s be darned.

> **TIP:**
>
> After your bid is accepted by the seller, hire an **inspector** to check out the property and structure and make sure there are no potentially expensive hidden problems. If so, you can negotiate the price down. It's $100 to $250 well spent.

After your down payment, lenders still require that you have enough cash in your bank accounts for a couple of mortgage payments, and that's *after* you pay closing costs.

**Closing costs** can be rough. You feel like you're paying everyone but the cleaning lady and for everything but the staples in your loan papers. What you *are* paying for is the final turnover of the property to you and all the fees and personnel that go with it.

You will need a **lawyer** for your close, so make sure you hire one early on and coordinate accordingly. Lawyers are a big part of the closing process. They make sure all the paperwork— from the titles to mortgages to your personal information—is tight, legit, and correct. This is not a good time to scrimp and do a close on your own (that is, unless you're a lawyer).

When a seller accepts your bid and your mortgage is in order, a whole background process gets started including your lender making sure the **title** is in order. The title is evidence of who legally holds the rights to the property. The lender has to make sure that the seller does indeed hold the title and therefore the right to sell the property.

The process continues with you handing over a deposit to show that you're serious to get the process rolling. This deposit will be held and turned over into your down payment when the home changes hands.

At this stage, in most states you will also receive a **Residential Purchase Agreement (RPA)** that spells out:

- The final purchase price.
- Full legal information on both parties (buyer and seller).
- The time period within which the sale must close.
- Any contingencies (such as if the seller knows a window is broken and gives you a credit for the repair).

**Important!** Make sure to close the deal by the date on the RPA or the whole transaction can be voided and you lose the home.

Before your closing, which is the day when you and the seller sign the final papers and complete the transfer of ownership, you should also receive a **good-faith estimate of closing costs** from your lender. It should give you a general idea of how much you'll have to have on hand on closing day, ready with a check.

**Closing costs can include:**

- Title insurance.
- Document preparation.
- Lawyer fees.
- Lender fees.
- Notary fees.
- Any property taxes due.
- Credit report fees.
- Processing fees.
- Underwriting fees.

> **COMMUNICATE!**
>
> You should be talking **every day** to someone who is a part of the process—your mortgage broker or your lender, your lawyer, the real estate agent.
>
> Be on top of the process and keep it moving!

**If you're buying a home with someone else, make sure your lawyer sets up either:**

**Tenancy by entirety:**

- Gives equal right of possession and right of survivorship for husband and wife only.

**Joint tenancy:**

- Two or more people have undivided interest and right of survivorship.
- Best if you're buying with your domestic partner.
- Similar to tenancy by entirety.

**Tenancy in common:**

- Undivided interest between two or more buyers.
- If one owner dies, the property must be sold.

Closing costs depend on the amount of your mortgage and what state you're buying in. For example, when we closed we had to pay several thousand dollars to the state alone for a onetime state closing fee (outrageous!). You can expect anything from **$1,500** to **$8,000** (or **1 to 7 percent** of the purchase price) in closing costs—and remember, a lender's good-faith estimate is, after all, an estimate.

However, if you're in a soft mortgage market (meaning that home sales are level or low), almost all closing administration fees (but not taxes) are negotiable. No matter the market, it can't hurt to ask a lender to go down on processing fees or document preparation fees.

At the close, make sure your signing hand is in good shape. You'll be signing your name more times on more documents than you've ever thought possible.

## HOMEOWNERS LOVE THE TAX MAN

When you rent, the money is gone and you get no tax breaks. Homeowners—especially first-time homeowners—can get a nice chunky tax break that makes a substantial difference in your bank account come tax time.

You'll be paying a substantial amount of **mortgage interest** over the life of your loan, but especially in your first couple of years of homeowning. So the feds give you a break.

As a first-time home buyer, all mortgage interest paid is a tax deduction (up to $1 million). And mortgage interest up to $100,000 on your second mortgage is also deductible. It doesn't stop there. The interest on a home equity loan (again, up to $100,000) is tax-deductible as is the interest you pay on a HELOC. On an average mortgage, your total tax deductions add up to thousands and thousands of dollars.

When it comes to paying points to a lender, you'll probably have to prorate the amount for the year in order to get any tax deduction. Tax laws on points are tricky—either hire an accountant or check out **IRS Publication 936** (at irs.gov) online.

Your closing costs and fees are, unfortunately, not tax-deductible.

When it comes to new homeowners and taxes, it may be worth the expense of hiring an accountant—you don't want to miss out on any potential deductions and tax breaks. You'll need that refund!

## READY TO BE A LANDLORD?

*Hey, you say, this home-buying stuff is easy once you get the hang of it. And there's money to be made!*

Yes, yes. All of the above may be true, but before making the move to buying another home as an investment and renting it out to tenants, ask yourself:

- Am I ready to get a call to fix a broken toilet at 2 AM?
- Do I know who will take care of the grounds, or shovel snow?
- Am I ready to dole out at least a 25 percent down payment, or more?

You've got to answer a hearty *yes!* to each of these to consider buying another home as an investment and for the rental income.

Truth is, lenders don't like second homes very much. Second (or third, et cetera) homes are a big financial risk, so lenders protect themselves by charging higher interest rates on second or third mortgages and also require a much bigger down payment. There will be no 80/20 or HELOC deals here.

But if you can swing the upkeep of the property, devote yourself to the job of being a landlord, and hold on for several years, the high costs (including possibly big renovation costs) of investing in another home can not only set up a nice wealth cushion for your future, but be personally satisfying as well.

## Web Links

**realestate.yahoo.com** Real estate information and news; rentals, new homes, real estate agents, and mortgages.

**money.cnn.com** The *Money* magazine and CNN site with a comprehensive real estate section, financing information, best places to live, and tips and commentary on buying and selling.

**craigslist.com** Find local apartments for rent or sale, or post your own "Wanted" listing.

**moversguide.usps.com** This is the moving information site of the U.S. Postal Service; you can change your address online and inform utilities when you move.

**goodmortgage.com** Mortgage calculators, tips, options, and information.

**bankrate.com** A consumer-friendly site with mortgage calculators, in-depth tools, and information on mortgages, credit cards, loans, and other banking information.

**mortgage-calculator.com** This site offers multiple mortgage-variation calculators, a rent vs. buy calculator, and an overview of the loan process.

**nationalmortgage.com** Lists of mortgage lenders, free mortgage quotes from lenders, tips on mortgage buying, and various calculators.

**fanniemae.com** Government-backed Fannie Mae is the largest national lender. The web site has financial products and mortgage lending and services for low-, moderate-, and middle-income families.

**freddiemac.com** For information on buying and owning a home, as well as mortgage options, this site helps homeowners and renters get lower housing costs and better access to home financing.

**irs.gov** The Internal Revenue Service offers information on taxes and tax laws. Look for info on mortgage and housing tax deductions.

**hud.gov**  The U.S. Department of Housing and Urban Development can give you information on lenders, brokers, and other home-buying tips. There are also links to government home-lending and -buying programs.

**myfico.com**  The site of the company that founded credit scores. Check out mortgage rates by credit score.

**domania.com**  A great site to check out local information on home sales and compare prices based on zip codes. You'll also find information and resources on mortgage rates, home value estimates, for-sale listings, and local Realtors.

**huduser.org**  Another HUD site, where you can view research reports on housing and economic and community development.

**nolo.com**  At this popular legal self-help site, look for help and information on various legal matters including landlords and tenants, and real estate.

**realtor.com**  Browse homes for sale and find mortgage calculators, loan calculators, housing market conditions, and neighborhood tours.

**dinkytown.net**  A great financial calculator site with various mortgage calculators.

**realtor.org**  The National Association of Realtors has information for home buyers and sellers.

**hsh.com**  This big publisher of consumer loan information offers mortgage stats, mortgage calculators, and info on other loans.

# 6

## The Need for Wheels

### *Car Buying, Owning, Financing, and Insuring*

Our beloved wheels.

They are tickets to freedom. They get us to our jobs. They perform weighty favors (as we lovingly drive too-drunk friends safely home), and sometimes get us some lovin'. But most of all—after the roof over our heads—our cars, for many a can't-live-without-it asset, can be our next biggest financial drain.

Unless you live where there is massive public transit to safely get you from here to there, it's almost impossible to function without a car. And damn, do we Americans love our cars. Right now, there are more than two hundred million cars, trucks, vans, and SUVs on the road. And according to *Money* magazine in 2004, that's not including the 3.5 million new cars sitting, unsold, in lots across the country.

Our relationship with cars is complicated and deep. There's no recognizing of the responsibilities and financial implications of buying and owning a car without giving props to just how emotionally tied we are to these machines. We don't need cars like we need other appliances in our homes, like a toaster. Our cars are an extension of our homes and an expression of who we are and how we live our lives. Cars are cool.

So, how to hook up a decent much-loved ride without ending up in a too-deep debt hole or, worse, straight-up wheel-less? The great news is that there are now, more than ever, great ways to score a seemly set of wheels, and once you're armed with some of the reams and reams of information available at your mouse-tip, you'll possess the power of a savvy consumer to get the right price.

## FIRST THE MONEY, THEN THE CAR

Before you even come close to a dealership or kick any tires, you have to figure out how much car you can afford. If you're reading this, I'm assuming a brand-new high-end BMW is not in your budget, but maybe an old-school, street-ready one is. And you're probably not going to pay for your car in full, in cash. But you need to know how much you can spend so you can shop in your price range and not get sucked into a budget-busting hot car at the dealership. So, as when buying a home, you'll need to calculate what you can afford to lay out up front and what you can afford to take out of pocket each month before shopping for a loan—and only then go shopping for a car.

Of course the amount of your monthly car payment is not the only wallet factor in sizing up your auto outlay. Keep in mind and tally up all the following expenses to get an idea of how much car you can afford:

**CREDIT BUREAUS:**

**Experian**
800-311-4769 or
www.experian.com

**TransUnion Corp.**
800-888-4213 or
www.transunion.com

**Equifax**
800-685-1111 or
www.equifax.com

- Car loan payment.
- Auto insurance.
- Gas.
- Parking fees.
- Maintenance (scheduled and unscheduled repairs).

Adding all these costs up can give you a better (and probably smaller) idea of what you can afford every month. A typical rule of thumb is to not spend more than **10 to 15 percent** of your monthly expenses on your car. That's a pretty tight budget to follow, but when it comes to a big bite like this, you want some flexibility in your budget to take care of any just-in-cases.

Once you know approximately how much you can afford to spend (and keep it conservative!), let's talk about getting that loan.

When people talk about **financing** a car, they're talking about how you're going to pay for it. This usually means taking out a loan. And just like with buying a home, taking out a big loan requires you to make sure your **credit reports** are in order. Get a copy of your credit report from the credit reporting agencies (see the box) and make sure there are no mistakes or black spots that are pulling your credit score down. Your **credit score** is the single biggest factor in how good an interest rate you're going to get on your car loan.

Your score can also be affected by how much available debt

you're using. If your debt levels (credit cards plus student loans and any other loans) are too high—say, more than 20 percent of your income—try to hold off getting a car until you can pay off some debt. Many lenders are more than happy to go ahead and **qualify** you for a loan that is much more than you can afford to comfortably pay every month. Keep your budget in mind and stick to that amount.

Besides a loan from Mom, Dad, or Uncle Joe, there are a few ways to get a loan for a car:

- A **bank, credit union,** or **lending institution.**
- The **dealership** (including captive finance companies, which are the financial lending branches of major auto companies).
- A **home equity loan** or home equity line of credit (**HELOC**).

It may seem easiest to walk into a dealership and have the folks there set you up for financing on the spot, but sometimes you can beat the interest rates offered at dealerships by checking out rates at top lenders at **bankrate.com** and other loan-comparison sites.

Dealerships would of course prefer that you fill out their financing forms when you decide to buy a car from them, but that's because most of these loans come from the manufacturers themselves (**captive finance companies**), and the dealerships make a cut on securing the financing for you; it's win–win for them. I'm not against the convenience of getting your financing from a dealership per se—it's especially hard to resist since they're always screaming about how "You can get 0 percent financing!"—but a good percentage of buyers don't actually qualify for these rates. Instead, play other banks and lenders against each other by getting several rate quotes and terms. In this way, you come out on top and can save a bundle every month by getting the best interest rate possible.

But the best thing about getting your loan from a bank, a credit union, or another prime lender before you go car shopping is that you can walk in and write the dealer a check— making it a **cash deal.** Distill-

**Don't tell lenders up front how much you can afford to pay each month.**

They'll lend you a higher total sum over more payments to fit your monthly budget—but the loan will be much more expensive.

**Instead, keep your total budget in mind and negotiate interest rates instead.**

ing your dealership transaction to writing a check means that you can bypass haggling out a down payment amount, interest rate, and monthly payments. There'll be no stuffing here—you'll see the full cost of the car up front.

Auto loans typically have a term of **three to six years.** Stick to that time frame as much as possible. Of course, dragging out your car loan to six or more years can help you afford a more

| $18,000 CAR LOAN AT 5.5%:* | | | | |
|---|---|---|---|---|
| Loan term: | 3 years | 4 years | 5 years | 10 years |
| Monthly payments: | $543.53 | $418.62 | $343.82 | $195.35 |
| Total # of payments: | 36 | 48 | 60 | 120 |
| Total payout at end of term: | $19,567 | $20,093 | $20,629 | $23,442 |
| *Not including applicable sales tax. | | | | |

expensive car—loan payments are stretched over a longer period of time. But you'll get hit with heavier interest payments, and by the end of the loan you'll have paid out much more than the original price of the car.

If you own a home, you can take out a **home equity loan** or **home equity line of credit (HELOC)** to finance a car. HELOCs are risky because their interest rates fluctuate; try to stay away from financing this way. It can look cheaper now because you can save maybe .5 percent, but down the road you can watch your payments rise sharply as interest rates rise.

If you're disciplined, a **home equity loan** can be a good idea mostly because rates are so low. With a home equity loan, the rate is fixed, and unlike a regular auto loan, the interest you pay is tax-deductible. However, the danger here is that these loans tend to stretch out over ten years or more, probably longer than you're going to have the car. This is a less expensive option only if you stick with making much higher payments than the minimum required and do your best to pay off the loan in three to five years. And make sure that you're not paying any fees! Lender fees can kill any savings you'd make with this type of loan.

You can take advantage of low interest rates, too, if you bought a car awhile ago and ended up with a high interest rate either because your credit wasn't as good then or Federal Reserve rates were high. Well, rates have been low for a long time, so (again, just like a home) if your credit record has gotten better, you can always work with a lender to **refinance** your auto loan. Just make sure that you don't pay extra **points** to get a lower interest rate or get hit with big fees. Refinancing works best if you still owe several thousand dollars or more—you can save *mucho dinero* in car payments, not to mention how much you'll save in interest payments over time.

## What Should I Buy?

So now you know how much you can spend. That means that though you wanted that new Lexus, your feet are back on the ground and you're ready to figure out what you need and what's available in your price bracket (not to mention a car you actually *like*). To get you started, ask the following:

- Do I want a stick (manual transmission) or automatic?
- Do I want room for passengers and/or cargo space?
- Where am I parking my car? Is it a big garage, or do I have to work with street parking?
- Do I do a lot of highway driving or city driving?
- Do I need four-wheel or all-wheel drive?
- Do I have a long commute or take road trips and need to be very comfortable?

Now's the time for some fun homework. Check out magazines and web sites for information on the cars that fit your specs. Make sure to visit **Edmunds.com,** Kelley Blue Book's web site **kbb.com,** and **IntelliChoice.com.** They have great tools for locating cars in your price range, across models and years. These sites also allow you to set up cars and their specs side by side for comparisons. The amount of information that's available to you now for car shopping is amazing.

What's also very important when choosing a car is its **resale**

**value.** It's hard to think about what a car is going to sell for when you're trying to buy it. But it's very important not only for when that time comes, but with regard to the **value** of the price you'll end up paying.

First up, realize that the bigger the discount you get up front, the bigger the hit you'll take on the price when you decide to sell. If a car needs to be heavily discounted, it speaks to its market value. Focus on moderately discounted cars or good deals for the make and model—not how much is taken off a sticker price.

Buying a car is not an investment. But if you don't run it into the ground, chances are you're going to need to sell it or trade it in someday. So make sure to research resale values on the cars in your shopping list at the sites I mentioned above. It means saving thousands of dollars on the back end.

## THE LOWDOWN ON LEASING

Leasing a car wasn't always a popular option. Now no one bats an eye. Lately, though, with interest rates so low and dealer incentives making car buying a good deal, the popularity of leasing has taken a dip. Still, manufacturers are starting to discount leased cars to reduce your monthly payment, so look for leasing to get back some love.

First off, what exactly is leasing and why would you lease instead of buy?

When you lease a car, you don't own it. You're paying a kind of depreciation, wear-and-tear fee to a manufacturer or dealer to keep the car for a specified amount of time, returning it with low mileage and in solid condition. Think of it as a home you rent. When you rent, you try to keep the place in good shape, knowing that after a specified amount of time, it's going back to its owner and it's no longer yours.

Leasing started off and remains mostly with luxury cars. Because monthly lease payments are usually less than those when buying (though remember, you don't actually own anything), it allows you to drive a better car for what your budget can afford. But leasing is now offered on nearly any make and model of car, with some monthly payments as low as $199. Though the low-cost pro of leasing may make that dream car of yours look like it's within your financial reach, the cons—or the limits of leasing—may not make it a smart option for you.

**Before considering a lease, ask yourself:**

- Am I okay with giving the car back (with nothing to show for it) after two or three years?
- Do I have a long commute or rack up mileage fairly quickly?
- Do I keep my car very clean, and inside foot traffic low?

The most expensive limit in leasing can be **mileage.** When you sign a lease, you're allotted a maximum number of miles you can have on the odometer at time of return. The mileage limit usually ranges between **10,000** and **15,000** miles a year. If your round-trip commute on weekdays alone is more than thirty miles or so, leasing is probably not for you—you'll rack up the maximum miles just going to and from work. If you return a leased car with miles above the limit, you will be charged 10 to 25 cents for each additional mile. That's a very expensive bill—going over your limit by just five thousand miles over a three-year lease could cost you an extra $1,250.

You will also be required to turn in the car in very good condition—it should need no significant repairs and should be shiny clean. Again, if you've lapsed here, you'll be hit with charges to bring the car up to the lessee's standards. You'll be charged for any damage to the body or excessive wear on the seats or interior.

And forget about making any additions to your leased car. No sound system upgrades or bigger wheels. You are required to keep the car as is, with **no modifications.**

Okay, so you're cool with the low mileage requirements, have no problem with keeping your ride spotless, and are disciplined when it comes to regular oil changes and maintenance. If so, you may be able to take advantage of not only the lower price of leasing, but also the fact that you can lease a car for **no down payment.** Of course, you can put some money down to lower your monthly payments, but leasing is one way of getting a car you want when you can't afford a down payment.

When you're ready to lease a car—this is after you've gone for test drives and checked out dealerships—your lease deal can be worked out over the phone and online. Of course, you could walk into a dealership and get a lease deal on the spot, but the smart and less expensive thing to do is pore through the leasing web sites available, such as **IntelliChoice.com** or **LeaseGuide.com,** and see what kinds of deals are available. When you've honed down the best deals, *then* call your dealer of choice and work out the deal over the phone.

Reading a lease deal can make your head spin, and learning the lingo requires a bit of homework. For example, what's considered a down payment is, on a lease, called a **capitalized cost reduction.** And the **gross capitalized cost** is the final negotiated price along with any fees or premiums.

Give yourself a rundown of leasing lingo by visiting **kbb.com** or **MSN Autos** online. This way, there will be no surprises, and dealers will know they're talking to a savvy customer.

Most leases are **closed-end** leases, which means you have to return the car at the end of the lease and pay a **disposition fee**—a charge for cleaning up the car for resale—with no further obligations to the lessee. But what if, after your lease is up, you'd like the option of buying the car? If so, make sure this is stated in your lease contract—ask for a **purchase option,** which means that you can opt to buy the car at the end of the lease for a previously agreed-on price (called the **realized value**). However, check to see if there is a **purchase option fee.** If so, and if it's a big one, it may not be worth including the option.

> To see how much the car you want would cost to lease vs. buy, go to:
>
> **edmunds.com** (decision calculator page).
>
> To take a quiz to see if you should lease or buy, go to:
>
> **acvl.com** (Association of Consumer Vehicle Lessors).

So you're pretty savvy on leasing and think it's the best option for you. Here are some tips on managing the leasing process:

- **Read your lease** through and through. Look for any hidden charges such as security deposit or service charges.
- Check the **insurance** rates on leasing the car you want. Leased cars have higher insurance rates—make sure you can afford it.
- Negotiate the **price** of the car you want before you start negotiating the lease. No need to mention that you're leasing until the price is set.

- See if you can **buy extra mileage** up front—to protect yourself if you know there is a possibility you may exceed your limit.
- Check out the cost of **breaking** your lease if you need to—it could be substantial.
- Treat your leased car extremely well so you can't get charged large **wear-and-tear fees** at the end of the lease—trust me, if they can, they will.

## THE ADVENT OF PRE-OWNED AND THE SHOCK OF DEPRECIATION

A favorite car writer of mine once said, "Buying new is for chumps." Why such harsh judgment, especially coming from a guy who drives and writes about new cars for a living? Well, that's because cars **depreciate** so quickly, you can turn around and in one year lose at least 20 percent of the value of your new car. After three to five years, your new car will lose 40 to 70 percent of its value, depending on the make and model. What other asset do you have that you pay, say, $25,000 or so for, and then turn around after a year to see it's worth a smidgen of the loan amount you're still paying off? Heck, your home value is at least going to go up with inflation. And your student loans have gotten you the education to get you a career with a salary that can keep rising. A new car, however, as big a money grabber as it is, can and will suck your bank account dry and only too soon down the road be worth half—or less—of what you paid for it.

Why buy new when you can get more car for much less money by driving a car that's only a few years old, runs like new, is completely backed by the manufacturer, and may even have that new-car smell? (It comes in a spray . . .)

What started in the luxury market as a way to lure new less affluent customers has become the norm for car companies. That's the practice of automakers and dealers offering **certified pre-owned (CPO)** vehicles. What a boon to car buyers.

CPO cars are used, usually low-mileage, "young" cars that have been run through a very thorough inspection (somewhere from 100 to 150 points) and refurbishment by a dealer, and then pass the standards of

> **CHECK OUT EDMUNDS.COM'S TRUE COST TO OWN (TCO)**
>
> The TCO shows you the "real" price of a car—a full tally of buying the car along with the cost of owning it over five years. You'll be surprised—some cars have prices that are lower up front but end up being more expensive to own over time than another model.
>
> **TCO takes into account seven factors:**
>
> 1. Depreciation.
> 2. Financing.
> 3. Insurance.
> 4. Taxes and fees.
> 5. Fuel.
> 6. Maintenance.
> 7. Repairs.

a manufacturer's warranty. Most CPO programs include cars that are no older than five years, have less than a hundred thousand miles on them, and have had no serious body or engine damage.

Cars that are CPO'd tend to average about $1,000 more than the usual price for the same car without the certification. But the tip-to-tail inspection and extended manufacturer warranty are usually worth the expense. The peace of mind alone can be tremendous. It's the difference between buying what looks great as is from a private sale, not knowing what's ready to pop out from under that hood, and knowing that you won't be spending money on repairs for the length of the warranty.

Buying a CPO car is the closest thing to buying a new one, but at a used-car price. Still, not all CPO programs are alike. Make sure to look into the inspection list and carefully review the offered warranty.

## BUYING USED AND TRADING IN

There is no shame in the buying-used game. You may not be able to afford an off-the-dock Benz, but you might afford an older— yet well-maintained—version. Plus, with so many cars coming off lease deals, there's a glut of "young" models that have low mileage and minimal wear and tear. And the prices on used cars have come down substantially in the past couple of years alone. In 2002, the average used car cost around $12,000. But in 2003, that price was down to $10,400. Good deal!

There are several ways to buy a used car:

- From a dealership.
- From an individual (private party).
- Online (for example, eBay).
- Certified pre-owned (CPO).

Buying a used car (that isn't certified pre-owned) from a **dealership** usually involves a service program or "after-market" warranty from the dealer, not the manufacturer. Because inspections are done to make the car suitable for sale under the dealer's name, expect the cost to be higher than what you'd pay if you bought the car from a private party. However, what you're paying for is peace of mind and service. It's up to you to decide if it's worth it.

**Online car buying** continues to become a more and more popular option—it gives you access to hundreds of cars (from individuals and dealers) that you might not see otherwise. Of course, buying a car from outside a dealership comes with risk, but there are sites that have been vetted and have good records for self-policing such as **Cars.com, Kelley Blue Book Classifieds (kbb.com),** and even **eBay.**

No matter if you find the car you want online or via the local classified paper, or you see it driving down the highway with its price written in soap on the window, buying from an individual can be risky—you're getting the car **as is.**

However, if you follow a few tight rules, you can be more confident with your purchase. A thorough run-through makes the seller know that you mean business.

**On the phone, before seeing the car:**

- Ask why the seller is selling the car (make sure you're cool with the answer).
- Make sure the seller is the one who holds the title of the car—ask!
- Ask for a rundown of any work that has been done or any accidents.
- Ask if the seller has all the car's maintenance or repair records and if it's okay for your own mechanic to take a look at them. (Sellers shouldn't mind—if they do, move on.)

When you call or e-mail sellers about a car, also ask for the **seventeen digit Vehicle Identification Number (VIN)** that's found usually on the dashboard, near the windshield. Take this number and go to both the **National Highway Traffic Safety Administration's (NHTSA)** site and **CARFAX.com** to run a search for the car's history, including previous owners and current title holder. This is great protection—you are making sure that the person selling the car is the rightful owner and can see if there are any shady records that give you a heads-up to ask additional questions before buying.

**When you check out the car in person:**

- Bring someone else with you. If you need to go alone, meet at a busy parking lot or service station to be safe.
- See the car in the daylight, preferably early in the morning so you can start the engine fresh and see how it turns over.
- Make sure the VIN matches the one you were given previously. If not, and it was only a mistake, don't buy the car without going back to your computer and doing a CARFAX and NHTSA search. If the VIN is way off or looks messed with, walk away.
- Don't let the seller make you feel rushed or hurried—take your time. This is a big decision.
- Make sure to bring with you a **flashlight** (to check under the car), a small **magnet** (to run along the body and check for nonmetal filler), a notepad, a pen or pencil, and some **paper towels** or a rag.

Also bring along a checklist of areas to review, such as looking at the **seams, tire tread wear, suspension, internal wear and tear** that matches the odometer reading (if there is heavy wear on the steering wheel and pedals, but the odometer reads thirty thousand, walk away!), and **smooth steering** and **shifting** when you take it for a test drive. You can find a great checklist at **kbb.com** (10 Steps to Buying a Used Car) or at **MSN Autos** (//autos.msn.com/advice).

Okay, so the car has passed your thorough inspection and your mechanic's inspection. One last step: Make sure you get everything in **writing** before

> ### A WORD ON CUSTOMIZING
>
> Sharp rims, extra chrome, fierce sound system . . .
>
> All fun and good, but what you like may not be what the next owner likes. Don't expect to get a return on what you spend on customizing.
>
> Spend your money on **more car** (faster, better, newer model), **less floss.**

you hand over payment. Write up a simple **contract** (if the seller hasn't already) stating all the terms, the amount being paid, whom the title is being transferred to and from, and how it is to be delivered. Remember, with a private sale, unless the car is still under warranty, you will be responsible for all repairs and maintenance from the payment and title transfer on. You've got that puppy as is, but if you've done it right, you just saved yourself anywhere from 10 to 20 percent on what you would have paid a dealer for the same car. Private car buying is work and a risk, but financially, your work pays off in the lower initial price.

## DEALING WITH DEALERS

*"Have we got a deal for you!"*

Um, not really. Dealers are going crazy trying to get cars off their lots. This is my precautionary segment that's mostly applicable if you're taking the plunge to buy a new car. Which, of course, you're only doing if you can afford not only the higher payments, but also the depreciation.

According to Cars.com, in September 2004 manufacturers offered an average $3,125 on **incentives** for every car sold. Incentives are discounts such as **cash-back rebates** and **0 percent financing,** and are becoming the norm in new-car sales. But think about it: You shouldn't be making such a huge purchase just because there's a big sale. As with retail, when something is marked down so low (or, in this case, marked down low by offering you cash back), someone's just trying to move the merchandise off the floor. The sale rack can be great for finding funky jackets, but when it comes to new cars you generally want to stay away from the super-duper-sale rack—it holds cars that they want to get rid of for a reason.

So what's better anyway, a 0 percent interest rate or a $3,000 cash-back offer? First of all, understand that just like with credit card offers, you may not qualify for 0 percent on your financing. But let's say you do. In that case, always break down what the monthly costs will be on each offer you get. You may be surprised which deal ends up less expensive over time.

Remember: Do you usually have to sell back what you buy on the sale rack? Instead of getting sucked in by these offers up front, think about what it will mean down the line when it comes time to resell your car. If it was worth less to the manufacturer at the outset, you can be darn sure it will be worth that much less come resell time.

> Q: Just how big has the car-sale rack gotten?
>
> A: **J. D. Power reported in 2004 that 63% of car sales involved some kind of rebate.**

I'll quote *Money* magazine here: **"If your new car starts life in the bargain basement, the only place to go is down."**

When it comes to **haggling** over price—whether you're buying new or used—your best weapons are found online. Find the:

- **Dealer's invoice price.** This is the dealer's cost for the car—the lowest price for which a dealer can sell the vehicle.
- **MSRP,** or the manufacturer's suggested retail price. This is the base sticker price set by the manufacturer.
- The **new-car Blue Book value,** from Kelley's Blue Book is a price or price range that reflects actual sales of your make and model. For a used car, look for **Kelley's suggested used retail value.**

It almost makes too much sense—but it's too easy to

---

**TIPS FOR DEALING WITH DEALERS**

- Tell them you're not buying today—**just shopping.**
- Don't tell them what you're ready to pay—instead, know what models you're looking at and keep a **sweet-spot price** in your head for haggling.
- Don't tell a dealer that you have **financing** already—get him or her down to a firm price first and *then* see if you're offered a better rate than what you've already set up.
- If you're feeling pressured, don't be shy—**walk out!**
- If you're a **woman** and the salesperson is not taking you seriously, ask to see the manager or supervisor—or better yet get moving to the next dealership.
- Shop around dealers and get prices from several on the make and model you want. **Play them off each other** to get the best deal.

forget—that as with any other merchandise, shopping during particular times of the year can get you better deals. For example:

- Shop for a convertible or sports car in the **winter.**
- Shop on the **last days of the month** when dealers have to make their monthly quotas.
- Even better, shop at the **end of the year** when this year's models need to move off the sales floor.
- Read up on when a make or model you like may be getting a complete overhaul in the next year (manufacturers usually redo models every six years or so). You can get a great deal on the **outgoing model**—but you may only want it if the upcoming changes are more cosmetic than anything. You don't want to buy an outgoing model that is getting a huge upgrade in safety features, for example. It's not worth skimping on safety.

## GETTING RID OF WHAT YOU'VE GOT

What if you're shopping for a new car, but you have to get rid of the one you have? Should you trade it in at a dealership, sell it to a used-car dealer, or set up your own private sale—or is it such a clunker that you'd be happy to donate it to charity?

### THE TRADE-IN ROUTE

Again, when working with a dealership, they have to make money. So you'll be paying for the convenience of having them take the car off your hands as is without you taking on any repairs or new parts to get the top price for your car. Trading in is a quick way to get rid of your car and drive home in another car that same day. If losing the extra money you might expect from selling the car yourself—anywhere from a few hundred to a few thousand dollars—doesn't hurt so much, go ahead and trade it in. But make sure you get a good deal.

Getting a deal on trading in may not happen. But if you

> ### DON'T GO UPSIDE DOWN!
>
> If you still owe money on your old car, don't roll the remaining debt into your new car loan.
>
> **It's a rolling debt trap, aka an upside-down loan!**
>
> **Instead, pay off your old car or trade down to a cheaper model so you don't end up taking on two loans instead of one.**

know how much your car is worth (again, check Kelley's Blue Book), you can try to haggle the trade-in price up a bit. And while you're shopping around at dealers for a new (or used) car, shop around for the best trade-in price. Does one dealer offer a cheaper price for the car you want but give you a really bad number for your trade-in? Maybe you'd rather go to the dealer who offers the car you want for a bit more, but gives you more for the car you already have.

Think about **trading in** as two separate deals:

1. What price are you giving me for the car I want?
2. What price are you giving me for the car I'm trading in?

Then subtract one from the other to see how much is coming out of your pocket for your new (or used) car. Whoever gives you the best final number can get your business.

Oh, and this is fun—in some states, instead of paying **sales tax** on the full price of the car you're buying, you can pay sales tax solely on the difference of the price of the car you're trad-ing in and the car you're buying.

## SELLING ON YOUR OWN

If you don't want to trade in your old car at the place where you're buying your next one, you can look for other car dealers that offer the same make as yours (say, Mazda for Mazda) or trusted local used-car dealers and have them sell your car. Re-member, though, that a dealer will usually offer even less for your trade if you're not going to buy a car there.

So if you have the time and energy to sell your old car on your own, you can make around **20 percent more** for what you have. And with great car sites on the web, or even eBay, more eyes can check out your car than ever before.

Selling on your own takes time. You need to take out your ads and put together a good selling package. You also need to prep your car to get it in selling order. That means performing any **maintenance** that needs to be done (oil change, tune-up), giv-ing it a thorough **cleaning** and waxing, and making any **repairs** that could possibly turn off buyers (upholstery, plugs, fans, tires, and so on).

Once your car is prepped and you've chosen some spots to list—whether online or in local papers or campuses, or both—you'll need to make the time to talk with prospective buyers and meet serious lookers. Are you comfortable vetting people? Are you a good haggler? Do you have the time in your sched-ule? If so, here's your chance to get some cash to apply directly to the financing of your next ride.

And make sure when you're ready to make a deal that the buyer is paying you either in **cash** or with a **certified check**. No matter who it is, you don't want to get a regular check only to see it bounce after you've transferred the title and canceled your insurance.

### You Can Always Give It Away

If you've got on your hands a real clunker, be generous. You can donate your car to charity and possibly get a tax deduction for the transaction. Check out **donateacar.com** for a list of charities that will accept your car and an overview of individual processes. Laws have changed regarding how much of a tax deduction you can get, but it can be a feel-good thing to do nonetheless. It's definitely better than sending it to the junk heap or dealing with some shady characters, especially if it's worth less than a thousand dollars.

## MAINTENANCE AND WARRANTIES

I know, I know. A warranty. Great, one more thing to pay for. But better you pay a bit up front than end up with a major engine part clunking out on you—in the middle of the highway, at night—and all repair costs coming out of your pocket. When you buy a car—new or used—you'll likely be getting it already under warranty for a period of time. If not, you'll have to shop for a warranty (also known as a **service contract**) that suits your needs.

If you're buying new, you'll be set up with a manufacturer's warranty (usually including **bumper-to-bumper, power train,** and **corrosion protection** for varying periods), so you'll be automatically covered for parts and labor up to a certain time.

Your new-car dealer may offer you an extended warranty or service contract as well, which you can reject with a clear conscience if you're not planning on keeping the car beyond the period that it's covered under the initial warranty.

But if you know you plan on keeping your new car beyond the warranty period, you may want to look into buying an **extended warranty** that will kick in once this happens. Extra money spent on an extended warranty is good to have even if you end up selling your car sooner than you think. It's worth a lot to a potential buyer and can get you more money for your car.

Truth is, what is termed an extended warranty is more like an insurance policy and service contract. What you're paying for is a separate maintenance policy—not included in the initial price of the car at point of purchase—to cover possible repairs and/or maintenance.

### How to Shop for a Warranty

First, you have to think about how much **coverage** you're interested in buying. Are you happy to pay a higher price for another bumper-to-bumper policy? Or are you okay with **breakdown** coverage?

Next, check out where you can buy a warranty, or coverage. You can get these from a dealer, a service shop, a manufacturer, or an independent company. There's no need to fly blind here. **Ask your local dealer or maintenance shop for a recommendation.** These guys and gals deal with warranties all the time and will know which companies are the easiest to deal with on both ends. Go with the recommendation, along with a quick look-up of the company on the **Better Business Bureau** web site (**bbb.org**).

Once you've chosen a company, review what it's offering:

- Will the company pay the service shop directly, or will it be reimbursing you afterward? If you're on a tight budget, **having the shop paid directly** can be a big plus.
- What's the **deductible**? And is it applied to **each visit** for service, or for **each repair**? This makes a big difference when it comes time to get multiple repairs done.
- Is the warranty **transferable** to the next owner if you sell the car before the warranty expires?
- Are **diagnostic visits** covered? What is **excluded** from coverage?
- Are **roadside assistance, towing,** and/or **rental car charges** covered?
- Are there any restrictions when you're **traveling**?
- Will you have to have all the repairs done at a **designated shop,** or can you choose your own?

How much coverage you need is up to you and what you feel comfortable with. If you have a car with a great reliability record and history, you may not want to pay for a bumper-to-bumper policy. But it's always a good idea to go with a policy that's **flexible** with the locations you go for service and with a deductible that is applied to **each visit** rather than each individual repair.

Regular maintenance of your car is critical. Make sure to find out your car's **maintenance schedule** and stick to it—procrastinating on oil changes and maintenance is the biggest reason that some cars fail before their time. Preventive maintenance can save you from expensive repairs or paying a big deductible down the road.

### Is Premium Gas Worth It?

**Not really**

Premium gas does nothing more than up your power by 2 to 4 percent. Most cars automatically adjust to be as efficient as possible, no matter what type of gas you're using.

Also watch for any **safety recalls** or **technical service bulletins (TSB)** on your car. If a manufacturer is recalling your car because of a defective part, system, or even potential problem, you'll be able to bring it to the manufacturer for exchange or repair, at cost to them, not you. The manufacturer does not automatically cover repairs needed because of a TSB, but if you have a good relationship with your dealership, it may be willing to do the repairs on its own tab.

Manufacturers love loyal customers and don't want unhappy buyers incurring major repair costs for something that was found out to be a mistake at their end.

## Auto Insurance

If you think your car payment is expensive, have you seen auto insurance rates lately? Actually, the rate that they've been going up has slowed down a bit (up only 3.5 percent in 2004), but there is no doubt that you'll probably be paying on average $1,100 a year or more to insure your car—and in many places much more. That can be another $100 or so a month on top of your car payment, gas, and maintenance.

Most states require insurance, and though it's another semi-painful expense, it no doubt helps you in the long run. It can prevent you from ending up in the poorhouse if you're in an accident and hurt someone badly, or if you hurt yourself and total your car. Of course God forbid this ever happens, but that's exactly what insurance is: coverage for the just-in-case.

> **REMEMBER . . .**
> - Check out insurance rates *before* you buy a car.
> - Be able to comfortably afford both car payments and insurance.

How much your insurance costs will depend on many factors. These factors get weighed by insurance actuaries, who then determine the likelihood that you'll end up filing an insurance claim. This is your **insurance risk score.** Yes, another score! This one sets how much you'll be charged for insurance. Factors include:

- What is the **make and model** of your car? If you drive a two-door sports car with lots of horsepower, expect high insurance.
- Where do you **live and park** your car? If you live in an urban area and park your car on the street, insurance will be high.
- What is your **driving record**? More accidents and/or tickets equals more cost.
- **Who else drives** the car? If you share the car with your teenage sister, you'll pay more.
- Does your make and model have a **good safety record and features**?
- Do you pile up a bunch of miles with a **long commute**? More time on the road means more money.
- Yet again—how's your **credit history**? Insurance companies have found that the better your credit history and credit scores, the less likely you are to need to file an insurance claim.

## AUTO INSURANCE SHOPPING

Shopping for insurance is another exercise in price comparos and patience. Again, the web to the rescue—there are some great sites that do the comparison shopping for you. And though you'll find only a range of costs, not an exact price, you'll get an idea of what you'll be sending to Acme Auto Coverage every month so you can budget accordingly and possibly rule out makes or models that have very high insurance premiums.

Before you start your shopping, it's good to know that there are a few different types of companies that sell auto insurance. Your insurance company type can tell you a bit about the who and how of your agent, broker, and middle person:

- **Independent insurance brokers** can get quotes for you from different companies. They sell insurance to you on behalf of the company you choose and sometimes charge a fee. Make sure they have certification from the Independent Insurance Agents and Brokers of America (visit iiaa.org) or the National Association of Professional Insurance Agents (pianet.com).

- **National insurers,** such as State Farm and Allstate, have a big employee pool of local insurance agents (called **captive agents**). You'll get one quote.

### HOW TO KEEP YOUR INSURANCE RATES DOWN

- Look for discounts (through your employer or club/affiliations).
- Arrange for a higher deductible.
- Drive as safe a car as you can afford.
- Drive safely—no accidents and no tickets.

- **Direct insurance brokers,** such as Progressive and Geico, eliminate a middle person. They sell insurance to you directly and assign you a local agent. They're popular for giving online quotes from multiple companies, helping you find the lowest rates.

As with any purchase, you don't want to necessarily go with the cheapest—you want the **best value.** Choose an insurance company that is reliable, treats you well, handles claims in a timely manner (and hopefully, pleasantly), and has a great track record.

Check out the insurance companies on your narrow list at your **state's department of insurance** to see what their **consumer complaint ratios** are (this is how many complaints they've received for every thousand claims filed). This is a big factor in choosing your car insurance company. You don't want to go through the stress of a car accident only to have your insurance company and their nasty claims people add to your drama.

Your **local mechanic** or **body shop** can also be an excellent resource here. These folks deal with insurance companies and agents all the time. It's a great place to start your shopping— just ask whom they recommend as insurers and which has the best local agents and claim-filing records and procedures. They're sure to give you the uncensored, un-PC scoop.

And of course, before you sign up for any auto insurance, make sure to **read your policy!** Hopefully, you'll only need to read it once, but doing a thorough scan before you sign on the dotted line gives you the chance to change anything in the policy you don't agree with, or even move on to your next choice. Protect yourself—read.

When you review your policy, you'll want to keep an eye out to **make sure you can still sue.** You should always keep your right to sue an insurer in case there is a big disagreement. If there is a statement or clause in your contract that asks you to give up this right, get it taken out.

One more step here: What kind of insurance and how much do you need? There are boatloads of types of insurance you can buy, and some that you are required to have:

- **Liability insurance** is required by most states—you can't drive without it. It covers property damage or injury that you cause in an accident. It can be separated into **bodily injury liability** and **property damage liability.**
- **Collision insurance.** On new cars, lenders typically require this to cover potential repair costs. It covers damage in a car crash, no matter whose fault it was.
- **Comprehensive** includes non-accident-related coverage, such as that for theft, vandalism, or weather-related damage.
- **Medical** and **personal injury protection.** If you don't already have medical insurance, you may want to get this—it covers your medical bills (and those of any passengers in the car) if you're in an accident. It also can protect you if you're hit as a pedestrian.
- There is another type of insurance that only applies if your car is totally lost (it's swept away in a hurricane, for example) and the amount that you're slated to get back

> Check out Kelley Blue Book's list of the **highest- and lowest-priced cars to insure** (by category):
>
> **kbb.com**

to replace the car from your collision or comprehensive policy isn't enough to cover your remaining car payments. **Gap insurance** is there to cover the gap—if there is any—between the amount you'll get from the insurance claim check and what you still owe for your balance of car payments. This insurance is most important if you're **leasing** your car.

- And there's one type of car insurance that you probably don't need to sign up for: **rental.** When you rent a car, you'll be asked to sign up and pay for additional insurance coverage. However, check out your own auto coverage, because it most likely extends the same coverage to a rental car. Also, if you pay with a credit card (especially gold or platinum), your card company usually has collision coverage for rentals. Check it out before you get a rental— you'll probably save yourself some bucks.

Remember, the insurance industry is a necessary behemoth, but its job is to prey on fear and what-ifs. So know what you need going in and you won't be taken for a ride signing up.

## Web Links

**insweb.com** A nationwide comparison site for insurance, including auto, life, and health.

**eloan.com** Information on loans for new and used (dealer or nondealer) cars and leasing a vehicle.

**capitaloneautofinance.com** At Capital One bank's site, check loan rates, calculate loan information, and apply online.

**carsdirect.com**  Get prices on new and used cars, look over a certified pre-owned vehicle guide, or buy a car at this top car-buying site.

**cnnmoney.com/autos**  The *Money* magazine and CNN site. You can research cars and find commentary and advice on car buying, leasing, and selling; tips on car buying and maintenance; financing information; and auto insurance info.

**progressive.com**  This auto insurer's site lets you compare rates, get quotes, and buy insurance.

**geico.com**  Shop for auto insurance, receive quotes, and make payments online. (We all know the funny commercials.)

**edmunds.com**  A top car info and buying site. Look for car prices and reviews, info on new cars, and how-tos for buying and selling used cars. It also features a finance and insurance center.

**kbb.com**  The Kelley Blue Book site is a top spot for info on new-car prices, used-car values, and free record checks.

**cars.com**  This big car-buying and -selling site lets you research, buy, and sell cars; it also features current automotive news.

**intellichoice.com**  Information, prices, and reviews on cars; leasing options and tips; car comparisons; and top-ten lists.

**leaseguide.com**  This consumer guide to informed car leasing offers lease calculators, guides, and other resources.

**msnautos.com**  Auto news and reviews, as well as a helpful glossary of leasing terms and insurance info.

**acvl.com**  The Association of Consumer Vehicle Lessors site features info on leasing a car and comparisons with buying.

**carfax.com** The site to find vehicle history reports via VIN numbers. It also lets you locate a dealer or car.

**nhtsa.com** The National Highway Traffic Safety Administration's site has vehicle and equipment information, statistics, tips, and news on car safety and recalls.

**ebay.com** Buy or sell your car or car parts online.

**donateacar.com** This car donation and charities center lists charities that will accept your car and tells you more about their missions.

**bbb.org** The site of the Better Business Bureau. Check up on a car dealership to make sure it doesn't have too many complaints filed against it.

**iiaa.org** The site of the Independent Insurance Agents and Brokers of America. Make sure your auto insurance broker is registered and has certification.

**pianet.com** The site of the National Association of Professional Insurance Agents lets you check up on your auto insurance broker or agent.

CHAPTER

# 7

# Honor the Tax Man

### *But Know How to Play His Game*

*"Thinking is one thing no one has ever been able to tax."*
—Charles F. Kettering

Let's face it: The words *fair* and *taxes* are probably not bunk-mates. Truth is, as much as we are disturbed by how much of what we earn disappears before we ever see it, taxes pay for the infrastructure of our lives—roads, police, bridges, fire stations, libraries, Medicare, and more, much more. Almost everyone, everywhere, who earns money is personally familiar with taxes. They may not pay taxes (Al Capone, Leona Helmsley anyone?), but they know what they are and what they're used for.

Interestingly enough, 2004 saw the lowest tax rates in thirty-seven years. According to the Tax Foundation, by April 11, 2004, Americans had earned enough money to pay off all their taxes for that year. In the past, that was a depressing (or liber-ating) day in May—farther in the year. Federal taxes have gone down quite a bit since 2000, but we can be sure that they'll never go away.

Most people's problem with taxes is how they get to be so high and who says what money pays for what. If you want to put your money where your mouth is, show up at the polls to vote.

In the meantime, accept the government in your paychecks— for a typical household, it's about a third of take-home pay— but make sure you know how to take what's yours in deductions and credits. After all, it's your money first.

## How Your Pay Gets Played

It's a bit of a shock when you get your first paycheck at a new job, or after a raise, and you see just how much difference there is between your **gross income** and your **net pay**. Where'd all that money go?

Well, your gross income is based on your salary, but you can pretty much forget about that number on a day-to-day basis, because you'll probably never see it. What you net, or actually take home, is your gross pay after taxes.

The feds know how much you make and how much to deduct from your paycheck because when you start a new job (a legit job, ahem) you are asked to fill out a **W-4 form.** This form asks you to fill in your personal information, along with your **tax ID,** which is your Social Security number, and how many dependents you have. If you're single, you enter a "1" and your final **personal allowance** will be 1. Now, this number acts as a guide telling the IRS (Internal Revenue Service, aka the tax police) how much to deduct from your paycheck in taxes.

If you enter a "0," you will have the highest amount for your tax bracket taken out of your paycheck since you're not taking any personal allowances. You'll probably end up with a big tax refund after you file because you've paid too much in taxes. If you enter a "1" because you are a single filer, you will get closer to the right amount deducted from your pay. However, if you are a single filer and you enter a "2" in order to have less tax taken from your check, you may owe quite a bit at the end of the year. My advice is to stick to a "1" if you're single and enter what you need to for any dependents if you have them—you'll be a "2" if you're supporting a child, add to that if you're the head of a household, and so on.

Folks seem split on the **tax refund** question: whether it's better to overestimate your taxes and get a refund, or pay close to what's right and possibly owe a bit. A refund can be a great check to get every spring, but if it's too big, it's your money that the government was holding for you when it could have been earning interest or spent on other necessities during the year.

However, my feeling is that when your pay is fairly low or midrange, and you'd probably end up spending that money anyway (you know who you are), it may not be a bad idea to let the government do the job of holding on to some of your money for a year, then giving it back to you in a lump sum to pay off a credit card, or open a savings or investing account.

> **I'M LATE . . .**
>
> - If you think you're **owed a tax refund** that you never received, you have **three years** from the tax date in question to file a claim.
> - If you were **due a refund but didn't file** your taxes, you have **three years** from the date your tax return was due to file a return and get your refund.

But if you gear yourself up every year to get that tax refund—spending it ahead of time because you know it's coming—better to cancel that sucker out and get yourself to pay more taxes up front by arranging for more withholding from your paycheck. Either way, what you definitely don't want is more than a couple of hundred dollars of your money floating around in government coffers. That's too much.

**And don't even think of *not* filing your taxes.** If you've filled out a W-4, or even if you didn't but your employer has filed and reported you as an employee, the IRS will track you down. And the penalties are painful:

- Daily compound interest is charged on any unpaid tax from the due date of the return.
- If you file on time but don't pay all you owe, you'll have late payment penalties of .5 percent of the tax owed for each month—up to a maximum penalty of 25 percent of tax owed.
- If you don't file and owe taxes, your penalty goes up to 4.5 percent of the tax owed each month, up to five months.
- If your tax return is more than sixty days late, the minimum penalty is either $100 or the tax you owe (if it's less than $100).
- And as Al Capone found out, the ultimate charge for evading taxes is jail time!

## Paycheck Play-by-Play

**Federal withholding** is probably the first minus line on your paycheck. This is the federal government's estimate of what you owe in taxes based on your salary. It is an estimate, which is why

| FEDERAL TAX RATES BASED ON INCOME FOR 2004 (SINGLE FILER ONLY) | |
| --- | --- |
| Income | % Tax |
| $0–7,150 | 10% |
| $7,151–29,050 | 15% |
| $29,051–70,350 | 25% |
| $70,351–146,750 | 28% |
| $146,751–319,100 | 33% |
| $319,101–up | 35% |

we have to do our taxes every year (well, it also gives us a chance to claim deductions and lower our federal withholding—more on this soon). Since our federal taxes are based on a graduated system, the amount we are taxed goes up according to our income, and the income bracket we are taxed at changes a bit depending on our marital status when filing.

The six tax bracket rates for 2004—which are quite a bit lower than a few years ago—are set to expire in 2011.

Also in the paycheck box that breaks down the deductions from your gross pay, you'll see **FICA** (Federal Income Contributions Act), which has been around since the 1930s. FICA is your contribution to Social Security and Medicare. If you make $87,900 or less (as of 2004), FICA takes **7.65 percent** of your gross pay (6.2 percent goes to Social Security and 1.45 percent to Medicare). Your employer contributes as well by matching that amount for every employee.

Of course, heated talk in political and financial circles is escalating, because the fund for Social Security (that our FICA taxes finance) is slated to start going into the red in 2030. That's not a long way off—so we can only hope (and vote) that something will be done to fix the system so that the taxes we pay toward this fund are there for us when we need them, at age sixty-two or later. In the meantime, we pay away.

Another tax that gets pulled from your paycheck may not be

applicable to everyone—**state** and/or **local city income tax.** There are still some very tax-cheap states to live in where no state income or local income tax is taken from your paycheck. For example, awhile back my dad got a job transfer from New York City to Massachusetts. He chose to buy a house in New Hampshire, commuting an hour to work, rather than paying Massachusetts state income tax. Interesting choice for him you might say, but I can tell you—living in New York City—that getting hit with both state and local income tax really adds up.

The bright side of this extra tax bite is that the feds allow you to deduct what you pay in state and local taxes every year.

## TAX TIME: RULES, OPTIONS, AND PAPERS

Thank goodness we no longer live in a time when taxes have to be filled out each year with a pencil and desk calculator. If you want to witness a firsthand exercise in bureaucracy (more like bureau*crazy*), take on a long-form, old-fashioned paper tax form. You'll be slammed on the head with reams of paper, wacky accountant-speak, and, if you can imagine, more than six thousand pages of tax code. And if you need filing instructions, be ready to review a healthy hundred pages and twenty worksheets.

Well, no need for that. When you do your own taxes, filing has become a much easier process. You can either purchase tax software from folks such as **Quicken** or **TurboTax,** or from large accounting firms such as **H&R Block.** No desire to shell out the $19.95 or so? The Internal Revenue Service now has a **free e-file** program letting you file your taxes directly online at **irs.gov.** The IRS's tax prep program is not as user-friendly (or amusing) as the software offered by other companies, but you know you're working with the source.

Besides the software to do your taxes, what you'll need is a **W-2,** which comes from your employer in January of each year—and from anyone else who paid you in the calendar year and reported your pay. Your W-2s have the basic information you need to file your taxes. If you have any income earned from interest or investments, you'll also receive a **1099** or other forms to report this income. Later in this chapter, I'll let you know what other papers you'll need if you have enough applicable deductions to itemize.

Before getting into what kind of tax forms you should use, you need to know your **filing status.** Your tax filing status is the other factor besides your income that determines how much you will be taxed. Here are your options and the standard deduction you'll receive with each status (as of 2004):

- **Single.** It's just you making your way, no one else. But if you are taking care of an aging parent or another relative, you may want to file as head of household (see below). Standard deduction: $4,850.
- **Married, filing jointly.** You're married (or got married anytime that calendar year), separated, or your spouse is recently deceased, and want to have all incomes and deductions treated together as one total. Filing jointly used to trigger a "marriage penalty." Thankfully, in 2001 a bill gradually eliminating the marriage penalty (HR 4181) was signed and put into law. Amen to that. Unfortunately, in December 2004, the law was set to expire. As I write, the

date has been extended to January 1, 2011. Standard deduction: $9,700.

- **Married, filing separately.** You're married but prefer to file your taxes on your own. This is an expensive option because you'll each be subject to higher tax rates. However, it may be a less expensive choice for you than filing jointly if one of you has a much higher income than the other and any deductions or credits you'd want to file wouldn't be allowed because your combined income would be too high. So if one of you went back to graduate school and/or had a load of medical expenses one year—and therefore also didn't have much income—you'd want to file separately so the deductions and/or credits qualify on the lower salary. But if one spouse itemizes deductions, you both need to. More on deductions soon. Standard deduction: $4,850.

- **Head of household.** If you're a single parent, or are taking care of an elderly parent or another family member at home, you want to file as head of household—you'll get a lower tax rate than filing as a single because you're taking care of someone. There are restrictions, however. If you are caring for an adult at home, he or she must have lived there for at least six months of the year you're filing and must have contributed to at least half of your housing costs. It gets complicated, so if you think you qualify, go on irs.gov and check out **Publication 17.** Standard deduction: $7,150.

- **Qualifying widow(er) with dependent child.** This filing status applies if your spouse passed away a year previous to your filing year and you haven't remarried (yet). Standard deduction: $9,700.

Once you know your tax filing status, you'll need to choose which tax reporting form you'll use. There are **three kinds of forms** available to file your taxes. Each has restrictions, and sometimes, even when the easiest form seems most appealing, another form will result in a smaller tax bill and therefore a possible refund. Most online tax prep programs and software can automatically check which form will net you the lowest tax bill.

- As the name implies, the **1040EZ** is the easiest tax form available. But you can only use this form if you are filing as single or married filing jointly, your income is less than $100,000, and you don't have any grants, scholarships, or earned interest over $1,500. On this form, you also can't claim deductions for an IRA account or for student loan interest.
- The **1040A** is a step beyond the EZ and has some of the same restrictions, including a taxable income no higher for the year than $100,000. As well as with the EZ, this form does not let you itemize any deductions. But on this form you can claim any IRA deductions, student loan interest deductions, and tuition and fees or educator expenses. You can also claim some tax credits such as for a child or children, and dependent care.
- The good ol' **1040** is the most complicated form (it allows you to itemize all your deductions and credits, one by one), but many times it's the most worthwhile—it allows you to fully claim all deductions and credits, resulting in a lower tax

bill. If you have deductions and claims that can make a difference in how much tax you owe, I highly recommend using this form even if your income qualifies you for an easier form. The money you get back will make it well worth the extra time. If you (or, if filing

> **!**
>
> If your crazy spouse has done something horrible like running out on you while owing mega tax dollars, you can protect yourself as an **innocent spouse.**
>
> Go to **irs.gov/individuals/** for the how-to.

jointly, you and your spouse) have a combined income of $100,000 or more, you *must* use this form to file.

If you're still not sure about your filing status or which form you should use, you can always visit **irs.gov** and pull up **Publication 17,** which will guide you through the full process and laws regarding your tax return.

And if you're doing your taxes yourself, it's a good idea to visit **irs.gov** and pull up any changes to the tax code or laws for the year you're filing. The link will be listed on the home page. It's difficult to keep track of this boring blather sometimes, but for such things as the marriage penalty, changes in tax codes and procedures can mean a big difference in what you owe, what you'll get back, or how you file.

## Basic Filing Tidbits

You may be surprised to know (or maybe not) that the most common basic—yet usually innocent—mistake people make when filing their taxes is messing up their personal information or those of other household filers.

> **!**
>
> If you owe taxes, make out checks or payments to the **"United States Treasury"** . . . *not* the "IRS."

Seems obvious, but make sure to **triple-check your personal information** on your tax form. That means especially your Social Security number—which functions as your tax identification number. A wrong Social Security number can send your refund to someone else or, worse, trigger an audit. And we know you want to avoid that!

With all this online e-filing, you'll also want to check over the information you enter for a **direct deposit** of any tax refund. This is another great plus of not only doing your taxes on your computer, but also filing them electronically. It gives you the option of getting your tax refund sent to you or deposited directly within a couple of weeks, rather than the snail-mail way of old that left you sitting by your mailbox for a month or more as everything was processed by hand.

And if for some reason—you're out of the country for a long time or just plain procrastinating—you can't file your taxes by the April 15 deadline, you can file for an **extension.** Though filing a tax extension (look for form **4868** at **irs.gov**) gives you another automatic four months within which to file, if you owe any taxes they are still due on April 15 regardless of when you file. So if you think you'll owe taxes, make sure to send along a check for part of it or for the estimated total amount along with your extension papers. If you don't, when you do file you'll owe a penalty fee and accrued interest in addition to the taxes themselves.

If you need more than the four months allotted when you file an extension, you'll need to file form **2688** to get more time. Of course, if you're at this point, you may want an accountant to do your taxes for you.

## Even *You* Get Tax Breaks

You may not have any investments (yet), or own a home (yet), or earn a huge income (yet!), but you still probably have tax deductions or credits that you can take to lower your tax bill and put more money in your pocket.

There are actually scads of complicated tax deductions and tax credits, but what I'll review here are the ones that you're most likely to be able to include in figuring out your tax return. Remember, if you do plan on itemizing deductions and credits, you'll need to fill out form **1040**. Tax software packages and online services will ask you several questions early on in preparing your taxes to see if you have deductions or credits that can lower your taxes and will automatically jump to the correct form if so.

First off, what are credits and deductions?

### Credits
A tax credit directly reduces the amount of tax you owe. So let's say that according to the federal tax bracket scale and your filing status, you owe $2,800 in taxes this year. But if you can claim a tax credit for say $750, you'll only owe $2,050.

There are only a few tax credits that you may be eligible for:

- **The Earned Income Tax Credit (EIC)** is a credit for not earning a lot. Huh? Basically, because you probably need all the money you can get—more so than those who take home more—the IRS tries to cut you a break by offering you this credit (more like a quasi-refund) on your taxes.

To qualify, you need to have earned less than $11,750 (as of 2005) that year; if you're married, less than $13,750. If you fall into this category, you will get an EIC reduction on your tax bill of $399. If you have a child at home, the income cap goes up to $30,030; if you're married, $33,030. In this case, you'll get a credit of up to $2,662. The income cap and credit amount go up to $35,263 (or $37,263 jointly) and $4,400 if you have more than one child.

There are several restrictions on the EIC because when it came into effect, lots of iffy folks tried to take advantage, and most filers who included an EIC were audited or reviewed with extra scrutiny. So make sure you follow the procedures well if you choose to take this credit, because you can count on a few extra pairs of eyes checking it out.

- **The lifetime learning credit** is equal to 20 percent of any tuition, room, board, and expenses for higher education that you paid within the tax year. Higher education need not mean only college or graduate school—you can also get credit for nondegree courses you took. This credit is for a maximum of $2,000 per tax return, and you must be reporting an income of less than $42,000, with the credit phasing out from this level up to $52,000 (for a joint return, the credit phases out from $85,000 to $105,000).

- If you are supporting a child or children under seventeen years old at home (it can also be a younger sibling or other family member), you can claim him or her as a tax credit. This **child tax credit** has limits depending on your income and filing status.

Other credits include the **adoption credit, electric vehicle credit, and health insurance credit.** For additional credits or more information on what I've listed above, go to **irs.gov/tax-topics/** and click on **"Topic 600,"** Tax Credits.

## DEDUCTIONS

A deduction shaves off money on the income end. Whatever you claim as a deduction lowers the percentage of your income that will be taxed. So if you made $36,000 last year but can claim a deduction of $1,200 for state and local taxes, you will be taxed on an income of $34,800. Not as direct and fast acting as a claim, but extremely valuable to have nonetheless.

There are so many deductions available—big and small—it can make your head spin. But because of your age, income, and lifestyle, you may be eligible only for some. Still, it's worth checking out any deductible to see if you can get your tax bill down. Here are some deductions that you may be able to take:

- **State and local income taxes.** 'Tis true: If you do get hit with state and local income taxes, the full amount of what you pay is considered a tax deduction.
- If you're not claiming a lifetime learning credit (you can't do both) but have paid out substantially for school **tuition and fees** during the year and make less than $65,000 (or $130,000 for a joint return), you can qualify for a maximum deduction of $4,000. If your income is between $65,000 and $80,000 or if you're filing jointly, between $130,000 and $160,000, you'll be eligible for a max deduction of $2,000.

- **Student loan interest.** Well, thank goodness Uncle Sam at least pretends to like education so much. You can also deduct up to $2,500 of student loan interest (the loan has to qualify as a student loan, though—no personal loans or credit card bills allowed). This deduction phases out when your income rises to between $50,000 and $65,000—or $100,000 to $130,000 on a joint return.
- When you become a homeowner, you'll be surprised how much less you dread the taxman. All the **mortgage interest** you pay over the year is tax-deductible for first-time homeowners, and there is a very high limit of $100,000 for non-first-timers. Note that the interest you pay on a **home equity loan** or home equity line of credit **(HELOC)** is also deductible. **Points** you've paid on your mortgage are also deductible, but they are prorated over time and kind of tricky. If you plan on deducting points, talk to a tax pro.
- Homeowners, rejoice: You also get to deduct the **property taxes** you've paid that year.
- You are allowed to deduct **medical expenses** from your taxes only if they add up to more than 7.5 percent of your gross income. But the list of eligible expenses is good and long so make sure to add up every co-pay, contact lens, therapist visit, and other big tag items not covered by health insurance such as vision-corrective eye surgery. There are probably going to be a couple of years where you'll be able to take this deduction.

Smaller deductions but ones you may be able to take (they all add up, don't they?) include deducting **mileage** if you use your car for business; **teacher expenses; home office equip-**

ment; moving costs for a job change; tax prep fees and expenses; and charitable giving.

For details on these deductions, check out **irs.gov/taxtopics/ tc500.html**. You'll get a full, detailed list of all the tax deductions available for individual filers, instructions, and limits of eligibility (take care to read through "Miscellaneous Deductions"—those magazine and newspaper subscriptions that you need for work but don't get reimbursed for can cut down your tax bill). Better yet, if you use tax prep software, you'll be asked in plain English about each deduction available to you so you have a chance to automatically include them in your return. The key with deductions is that you can't claim them if you don't have a receipt. Keep your receipts for the year safe so that come tax time, you have the paperwork to file your deductions.

### Tax-Free Stuff

So we've got tax credits and deductions. Things ain't lookin' so bad anymore, no? Well, there's still more you can do to cut down some of those dollars going to DC.

- **Scholarships and fellowships** are tax-free when used by a degree candidate for expenses at an eligible school.
- **Employer-provided educational assistance.** Your employer can give you up to $5,250 in educational benefits a year, and the course work doesn't even have to be work-related.
- **Canceled student loans.** Even though most canceled loans are taxable, if you were able to cancel your student loan (see chapter 3) because you've worked for a certain time at a qualified nonprofit organization or inner-city school, you won't have to pay taxes on it.

- **Health savings accounts (HSAs)** may be available to you if you have a high-deductible health plan from your employer. With these accounts, you can deposit and withdraw some of your income tax-free to pay for health expenses.
- You can contribute up to $4,000 a year into your **IRA** or **401(k),** tax-free. You pay taxes when you pull out the money, but as it goes in—and in many cases gets matched by your employer—it earns a return on a larger tax-free amount. Over the years, the tax savings exponentially outweigh the tax bite when you retire.
- **Capital gains from a home sale.** The profit you make on selling your home—up to $250,000—is tax-free as long as it was your primary residence (and not an investment or "landlord" situation) for at least a full two of the past five years. A mega $500,000 is tax-free if you file jointly.

## TIME TO GET AN ACCOUNTANT?

With all this online and software help, it's easier than ever to do your own taxes. However, there are instances where it makes sense and can save you money to have a professional do your taxes for you:

- Are you a homeowner or did you just buy your first home?
- Are you self-employed, acting as a freelancer or contractor?
- Do you work from home?
- Do you have substantial medical expenses, or did you lose your home to fire or flood?

- Did someone leave you a substantial inheritance tied to various investments?
- Do you trade stocks online or trade in various investments on your own?

Any of these can mean that it may make sense to pay an accountant or other tax professional to help you do your taxes. If you don't, you could be missing out on substantial deductions (did you know that the filing cabinet and/or television that you bought this year can be a deduction if you work from home or are self-employed?). A tax prep professional can squeeze out deductions that you wouldn't even think of. And why would you know? We're not tax pros—hand those files over and get what's coming to you.

To find a tax preparer, ask friends and family for referrals. You want to make sure to sign on with only the most trustworthy professional. After all, you're giving this person your Social Security number, personal contact information, and information on all your accounts. Vet this person well and take a referral from someone you trust.

You can also use a big company such as H&R Block to do your taxes. Staff at large firms are held to the privacy standards of any financial services company.

Just try not to show up on April 12 and expect to file on April 15. Whoever is doing your taxes no doubt has many others to do as well. Do your best to pull your files together (W-2s and 1099s, receipts, et cetera) and hire someone as early as possible. Most employers mail out W-2s in January, as do the holders of any interest-bearing accounts. If you wait too long to get your tax pro on the up-and-up, you'll need to file an extension. Give the gal or guy a break and get the process started by February.

That refund check is waiting for you.

## Web Links

**irs.gov** The site of the Internal Revenue Service (aka the Taxman), this is the mecca of all tax and tax-related info. It features changes to tax laws or new laws and codes; tax credits and deductions; and Q&As on tax forms and filing your taxes.

**quicken.com** The Quicken software site lets you purchase tax software and offers tax tips, resources, help, and support.

**turbotax.com** At TurboTax's software site you can purchase software as well as read up on information and guidelines for tax filing.

**hrblock.com** The site of tax-filing monster H&R Block offers advice and info about the tax filing process. You can also buy tax software and locate an H&R Block office near you.

**kiplinger.com/finances/taxes** The tax section of *Kiplinger* magazine's web site offers tax tips, advice, a tax form checklist, and other tax tools.

**taxadmin.org** The site of the Federation of Tax Administrators. Find state tax comparisons, links to state tax agencies, and other tax news and info.

**1040.com** This tax resource and information center has tax calendars, articles, a tax estimator, and filing info.

**officialpayments.com**   This is the site where you can pay your taxes online with your credit card (only if you really have to!). You can also get federal, state, and local tax information.

**money.com/taxes**   The tax section of *Money* magazine's site has info on tax essentials, advice and commentary, and tax planning and saving ideas.

CHAPTER

# 8

# The Golden Net of Insurance

## *Cover Your Ass*

*"The cautious seldom err."*

—Confucius

Ah, the invincibility of our youth. "It won't happen to me." "What are the chances of *that* happening?" "I'll deal with it when it happens."

Let's say the apartment upstairs floods, seeping into yours, waterlogging your computer, television, and stereo. Or you just happen to park in the wrong neighborhood when visiting your new friend from work—say bye-bye to your new car. Or you trip down the stairs, stopping your fall with your right hand, which then breaks your right wrist—ouch. Anything can happen.

Do you cross your fingers and hope it goes away? Unfortunately, it won't work out that way. But fortunately, you can pay a bit in advance to make sure the financial worst doesn't happen in the future. No need to compound the drama of what has already (possibly) happened.

That's what insurance is for. Think of it this way: You put a bit of money into a pool, and if and when something happens to you, your home, or your car, money comes out of the pool to help cover the costs.

Of course, we all wish it were that simple. But the concept is the same. Insurance is there to help cover you and yours when shit happens. The difference between paying every month to cover your health, home, and property and paying a $23,000 hospital bill can be the difference between freedom and financial ruin.

From having the money to replace your computer and sound system to recovering in the hospital and knowing that you're not destitute, paying for insurance is investing in peace of mind. Health insurance, rental or home insurance (see chapter 6 for auto insurance), and disability insurance can be amazing lifesavers—pain-in-the-budget though paying for them may be. And there are many choices and options when it comes to coverage. Read on and see what's best for you.

Always better to be safe than sorry.


## Health Insurance:
## What You Need and How to Find It

In nearly every other developed country, paying for health care is not something that gets a second thought—the government covers health care. Nonsocialist country that we are, however, health care either is a benefit offered by your employer or comes out of your pocket in the form of paying for an insurance policy, paying directly for services, or—in the case of very low incomes—turning to the government for help in picking up the tab.

> ## 1 out of 10
>
> . . . bankruptcies are caused by medical bills.

Lamentably, health insurance is not the norm for all young adults. According to the Census Bureau, adults age eighteen to twenty-four were the group least likely to have health insurance—almost 30 percent go uninsured, compared with 14.7 percent of the population as a whole as of 2002. And a little over 23 percent of twenty-five- to thirty-four-year-olds are also without health coverage. That's for a total of almost eighteen million young adults lacking insurance to help pay for anything from a basic checkup to a catastrophic illness.

If you have health insurance now, there probably was a time when you didn't. Maybe it was when you first graduated from college and got bumped off your parents' plan (been there). Or maybe it was when you got laid off in the internet bust of 2000 and didn't sign up for COBRA (more on that later) coverage, thankfully remaining healthy until you started your new job a few months later.

At any time, about 44 percent of adults go without health insurance for a stint of two to four months, and almost 20 percent are without insurance for five to eight months. It's a creaky bridge to cross—perilous, but very common.

Unfortunately, I've been too close to seeing how financially devastating it can be to go without health insurance. A couple of years ago, a younger sister of mine became ill and had to have surgery. She worked full-time for a small business and didn't have health insurance yet. To make matters worse, the surgery led to a major infection and additional operations that put her in and out of the hospital for days. And not only did she have no insurance and subsequently got hit with an incredible bill—even after the hospital decided to charitably swallow some costs—but she was out of work for a

> The uninsured die sooner than the insured. . . .
>
> —Kaiser Commission

month. My sister will probably be paying medical bills—on top of her student loans—for many, many years to come.

Your health is your most valuable asset. If you forgo insurance of any kind, let it not be health insurance. Not to get schmaltzy, but without health insurance you put at risk not only your financial future, but also your family or anyone who cares for you and would have to help you in case you were unable to work or to afford a place to live on your own.

You may already have medical coverage through your job. The Bureau of Labor Statistics reported in 2004 that 69 percent of full-time workers have access to health insurance from their employer, but only 53 percent of all workers participate in the health coverage plans available to them.

Why not sign up for a tremendous benefit that's offered to you? Of course the benefit is not totally free, and the trend is for employers to put more of the onus of health costs on employees. In 2004, the average monthly premium paid by an employee for single coverage under an employer's plan was $67.05; coverage for a family averaged a hefty $263.25. That's gone up a lot in only five years. Only five years ago, a single employee paid about $20 less and a family paid almost $100 less.

Health care ain't cheap, and unfortunately companies are squeezing as much as possible from employees to contribute toward their benefits. But I can't emphasize enough how much cheaper it is to pay your share for this benefit or even to get health insurance on your own than to pay for medical care out of your pocket.

So when you go to sign up for health insurance with your employer (**group insurance**), what the heck to do with all the choices available? You can pay this amount but not see that doctor, or you can pay that amount and see these doctors, or you can pay more and see whomever you want. Very confusing. Let's straighten this out.

Whether you're signing up for health insurance with your new employer, or you're looking to change the plan you have when it's open enrollment time with your current employer, or you're shopping on your own for health insurance coverage (**individual coverage**), there are basic types of coverage that you'll come across. Which you choose depends on your personal health needs. For example:

- Do you have an existing condition that requires you to go to the doctor often for medication and other procedures— asthma, allergies, diabetes, migraines, depression, or the like?
- Do you participate in risky activities such as RV riding, hiking, racing, or skiing?
- Are you pregnant or do you plan on getting pregnant soon (pregnancy always requires lots of routine care)?
- Do you have a doctor or two whom you've been seeing for years and want to continue to see?
- Do you use alternative therapies such as acupuncture or massage?
- Are you in very good health and happy to pay to go to a clinic when you're sick with minor ailments?

- Do you travel a lot and might you need to see doctors or specialists when you're on the road?
- Do you keep good records and tolerate paperwork and record keeping?

Your answers to these questions, along with how much you're able to pay, can help you determine what health plan is going to work best for you. Also, each plan comes with a different **premium**—the monthly amount you pay for your coverage. The semi-hard rule here is, the more freedom your plan gives you in choice of doctors and care, the higher your premium. **You pay for choice.**

## GROUP HEALTH COVERAGE OPTIONS

**HMOs (HEALTH MAINTENANCE ORGANIZATIONS)**
Once justly reviled for their restrictions, HMOs have made many changes over the years that make them a decent health care option today. HMOs are a form of **managed care.** You choose a **primary care physician (PCP)** from a roster of participating doctors, and any other specialist you see needs to be within the HMO network. Before seeing the specialist, you'll need to get a **referral** from your PCP. You may also need a referral for hospital procedures and will be limited to certain hospitals and doctors for coverage. (Though lately, in response to grumbling, many HMO enrollees are now able to see certain specialists—such as an ob-gyn—without a referral.)

As you can see, an HMO is limited. However, you won't have any claim forms to fill out. All you'll need to bring to the doctor is your enrollment card and $5 to $10 or so as a co-payment (your **co-pay** is a flat fee from the HMO for every visit or procedure). And your monthly insurance payments cover surgeries, diagnostic tests, hospital stays, and emergency room visits as long as they are within your HMO network.

## POS (POINT OF SERVICE) PLAN

This plan is very similar to an HMO: You'll have a network of doctors to choose from for routine care, along with specialists to whom your PCP can refer you. You'll pay a co-pay for every visit and hospital stay.

> **Unfair, but often true . . .**
>
> You may have to **wait longer** for an appointment if you're enrolled in an HMO or POS plan.
>
> The more **expensive** your plan, the **faster** you get to see a doctor.

The main difference between an HMO and a POS plan is that the POS plan allows you to see doctors outside the network— however, your coverage will only pay a portion of these costs. So if you have a specialist you want to see who is outside of the plan's network, insurance will pick up a portion of the bill, but you'll be responsible for the rest. The premium on this plan is higher than an HMO, since you're paying for the option to be partially covered when you go out of network.

## PPOs (PREFERRED PROVIDER ORGANIZATIONS)

Another network-type plan, PPOs give you just a bit more freedom than either an HMO or POS plan. Yes, you'll have a network of doctors and specialists to choose from and you'll pay only a co-pay to see them, but you won't have to deal with referrals. Paperwork with this plan is minimal, and if you choose to see a doctor out of the network, a portion of the cost will be covered; you're responsible for the rest.

You pay for the convenience of being free from having to get referrals with a higher premium, but it's a good option if you have a condition that requires you to see specialists often.

### Fee-for-Service (Indemnity) Plan

Close to being a thing of the past, this is the most comprehensive and flexible insurance plan available, but premiums and deductibles are expensive. This is what used to be traditional health insurance—you choose whatever doctors and/or hospitals you want and you're covered.

Well, mostly. As with all other plans, you'll pay a premium (pretty high), plus a deductible (ranging anywhere from $250 to $5,000) before the insurance kicks in. This type of insurance is actually a kind of co-insurance that depends on a ratio—so 80/20 means that your insurance will cover 80 percent of your health care costs (again, after deductible) and you take care of 20 percent. This can work out to be very expensive, but there usually is a **cap** (limit) on how much you pay out of pocket for the year before the insurance kicks in 100 percent for all of your costs for the rest of the year.

And you'll need to like paperwork—with some indemnity plans, you'll have to pay the bill up front then file for reimbursement.

### High-Deductible Plan Plus HSA (Health Savings Account)

Health insurance plans with high deductibles (we're talking $1,000 and up) are getting more and more popular, not only because their premiums are lower but because in December 2003, Congress created a crazy hybrid savings/investing/tax shelter account called an HSA (health savings account) specifically to help pay for this type of health plan.

If you're a young adult, this is probably not the plan for you since it requires putting up anywhere from $1,000 to $5,000 out of your pocket before your insurance kicks in, but just in case your health costs are very low and you can handle a potentially high deductible, I'll run through how HSAs can save you some money.

An HSA allows you to invest **pre-tax money** (straight from your paycheck) to cover health care costs, including everything from hospital visits to contact lenses to Claritin. You invest your money tax-free and withdraw it for medical expenses tax-free. And if other family members are covered by your insurance policy, HSA funds can be used for their health expenses as well. However, if you withdraw HSA money for anything else—say, retirement or a down payment—you will be taxed. You can put up to around $5,000 into this account every year, and it's invested like a mutual fund or 401(k). You can also keep your account when you change jobs.

The danger with a high-deductible health plan is that if you develop a chronic illness, you could end up paying your full deductible, year after year.

---

**CUSTOMARY FEES\***

You may have an in-demand doc who charges **$325** for an office procedure, but other doctors charge only **$175** for the same procedure.

Your insurance company calls the **$175** the customary fee and will reimburse your pricey doctor **only that amount—leaving you to come up with the rest.**

\*Applicable with fee-for-service or out-of-network doctors.

The difference between this savings program and its now lesser cousin the FSA (flexible spending account)—see below—is that you get to keep whatever moneys you don't use and let the account build from year to year. More on FSAs soon.

All this PPO, POS, HMO, PCP clatter can strain your decision skills, but answering one heavy question can narrow down your options: **What is most important to you when it comes to health care?**

- If you have allergies and need to get shots regularly, go with a **PPO** or **POS** plan so you won't be charged up the wazoo for your frequent visits to the same doctor.
- If you play sports and may need a hospital visit or two for field injuries, better steer clear of an **HMO** that can limit what hospital you can go to. Ditto if you travel often for your job.
- If you are very loyal to your family doctor and/or want to have the freedom to see any specialist of your choice, you may need a **fee-for-service** plan or pay extra out of pocket for a **PPO**.

Unfortunately, no matter what kind of benefits your employer has available for you, or what you're willing to pay for individual health insurance, the out-of-pocket costs of health care are going up every year. In 2004 alone, costs went up 14 percent. There are few basic quality-of-life necessities that have seen such a

> **For additional help choosing a health plan, check out this Q&A:**
>
> cgi.money.cnn.com/tools/ healthplan/healthplan_101.html

price explosion. The BLS reports that the percent of employees with group medical coverage who are required to pick up some of the costs went from 47 percent fifteen years ago to 69 percent by 1997. We're close to 100 percent now.

As I mentioned earlier, to help defray some of these costs Congress came up with a tax-free savings and investing plan—HSAs—with restrictions, of course.

Your employer may also offer another way for you to put away pre-tax dollars to help pay for medical costs: **FSAs (flexible spending accounts).** FSAs have been around for a while. Basically, at the beginning of the year, you fill out a form allowing for a certain amount to be taken out of your paycheck over the year—before taxes—to be placed in your FSA.

Then, anytime you pay for a qualified medical or health expense or deductible for you or a family member also covered by your insurance (make sure to read your FSA list to find out what qualifies), you send your receipt in to FSA processing and receive a pre-tax reimbursement from your account. If you're on a limited income, an FSA may seem counterintuitive—it takes more money out of your paycheck. The advantage, however, is that it's a type of forced savings account that yields you—depending on your tax bracket—anywhere from an 18 to a 30 percent return from the tax savings. That's tax money you wouldn't have seen otherwise.

And the list of reimbursable items can be quite extensive—contact lenses, prescriptions, aspirin, shoe inserts, Ace bandages, and co-pays. So if you have any conditions that require frequent trips to your local drugstore, an FSA may be the thing for you, no matter what type of health insurance you have.

Still, there are a couple of reasons why I'm not the hugest fan of FSAs:

- **Use it or lose it.** The money in your FSA must be depleted by the end of the year or you forfeit it—it disappears! It demands that you keep close tabs on your account and make sure that your receipts add up to enough to get back what's yours—or it's gone.
- **Paperwork.** You'll need to fill out forms and mail receipts (making sure you make your own copy in case they get lost in the mail) in order to get reimbursements from your account. If you've got the time and means to do this, all the better. But if you're overrun with paperwork for other things or your job, your FSA may get lost in the mayhem and you can lose money as you lose receipts.

## INDIVIDUAL HEALTH INSURANCE AND HEALTH CARE

Right, this is all well and good, you say, but you work for a small company (fewer than twenty employees) and it doesn't offer health insurance (because it doesn't have to). Or maybe you've just finished school and you're looking for a job—meanwhile, you're not covered. Or maybe you love your freelance/contractor/artist life and don't want to sign up to work for The Man, but you really need health insurance, just in case.

Well, you've got options, and you may be surprised to learn that you will be able to afford them.

## INDIVIDUAL COVERAGE

All of the health coverage options mentioned earlier (HMOs, PPOs, and so forth), which are offered in many group coverage plans, are also offered as individual coverage. Again, your health care needs and how much you can afford will determine what plan you end up with.

But because individual insurance costs substantially more than what you'd pay as a premium to an employer, you have some bare-bones options as well.

All the major insurance companies (such as Blue Cross) have plans for individuals. To get a comparison of available plans and your potential costs, visit **healthinsuranceinfo.net, eHealthInsurance.com, InsWeb.com,** or **Insure.com.**

You may not be able to pay $300 a month for basic health care coverage from a large provider, but if you're fairly healthy and willing to raise your deductible from the standard $500 to, say, three or four times that, your monthly costs can go down to around $50 a month—very affordable.

Also check out the doctor you choose as your PCP at places such as **thehealthpages.com** to make sure there are no discipline records or heavy lawsuits against him or her. This site can also help you find a PCP or other specialist if you're still searching.

If you're in very good health and don't regularly need to see a doctor, you may want to consider **catastrophic insurance.** This insurance has a very low premium because it will only cover you if you need medical care as a result of a catastrophe. Now, make sure you read exactly what the insurance company considers a catastrophe so you're clear on what will or will not be covered.

Hopefully you don't have a chronic health problem, because

if you do—and you're shopping for insurance—you may have a very hard time. Health insurance companies consider you high risk and as you probably know too well, as a result they probably won't want to offer you coverage. But don't despair—visit your state or local health department or agency web site (get a list of state sites at **cdc.gov** or **fda.gov**) and look for a local **high-risk insurance pool** that you can join for coverage.

If you're simply between school and getting a full-time job and just need insurance coverage for a short time to bridge the gap of a few months, check out your options for **short-term insurance coverage.** At the sites I mentioned above (and listed at the end of the chapter), you can search for options for short-term coverage. Short-term coverage will of course be less expensive than long-term coverage, so even if it's for only three or four months, it's worth signing on while you wait for your next gig.

Speaking of being between jobs . . .

## COBRA (CONSOLIDATED OMNIBUS BUDGET RECONCILIATION ACT)

If and when you're let go from a job where there are twenty or more employees, you are entitled to stay on your group insurance policy for at least eighteen months, but with the full enrollment cost covered by you. COBRA is a federal law that requires your former employer to offer you this health insurance option. The government put this law into action in 1985 to lower the numbers of uninsured—especially those between jobs, and

> If you **move** and your COBRA health plan is not offered at your new locale, **you lose your coverage**—your employer is not obligated to set you up with another plan in your new town.

their families. (This doesn't apply to individual insurance you purchase on your own, just group coverage.)

Now, whether you are laid off, quit, or are fired (except for "gross misconduct"), you are entitled to be covered by COBRA. If you're married and have children, your family is also covered under this program for a max of eighteen months. Or if heaven forbid you pass away or get a divorce, your spouse and child(ren) can be covered for up to thirty-six months.

COBRA coverage is a nice option to have, but unfortunately it ain't cheap. Since you'll be paying the full premium yourself, you can expect to fork over nearly ten times what you're used to paying when you were employed. But again, if you end up hospitalized without COBRA coverage, those couple of hundred dollars a month will seem like a pittance compared with your hospital bill.

COBRA does have restrictions. You cannot change the coverage you have at the time you became unemployed. You go out with what you had—no changes to your plan.

Your employer is responsible for informing whoever administrates the company health plan that you're leaving and has thirty days to do so. The administrator then has fourteen days from the day he or she is informed to contact you in person or by mail about your right to get coverage under COBRA.

Next, you have sixty days from the day you are notified to choose or waive coverage under COBRA. If you choose to enroll, you'll have forty-five days to pay the first premium, and your coverage will then go **retroactive** to the date you lost your original benefits. And you have a thirty-day grace period from your due date to pay your monthly premiums.

Still with me?

## HIPA (HEALTH INSURANCE PORTABILITY AND AFFORDABILITY ACT)

Say you've decided to forgo COBRA and shop for your own individual health plan. Well, here, another federal act comes into play: HIPAA. Even if you have an existing or pre-existing condition, if you've been covered under a group plan within the past sixty-three days, no insurer can refuse to offer you coverage. Now, you may not be able to afford what they offer you, but they still can't turn you down. If you have a pre-existing condition and need an individual policy, make sure to check out the **high-risk pools** I mentioned earlier.

### LOW-COST OPTIONS AND EMERGENCIES

But say you're really low on cash and paying a monthly premium is just not an option. There are always low-cost health care options, especially for children, so make sure to check out "People Looking for Low-Cost Health Care" at the web site of the **U.S. Department of Health and Human Services (//bphc.hrsa.gov).**

There are also many low-cost health clinics across the country—look for the one nearest you at **cdc.gov,** the web site of the **Centers for Disease Control and Prevention.** There you'll find links to your state health departments that list clinics in your area. For a broader search, a good portal to most government health agencies and initiatives is **health.gov.**

**Free clinics** may also be an option. For a complete directory of free clinics across the United States, go to **medkind.com.** On the home page, you can search for a free clinic by selecting the state you live in.

Especially if you're pregnant, make sure to seek out women's clinics that provide very low-cost or no-cost prenatal care.

If your take-home pay is very low and you don't own a home,

you may qualify for **Medicaid.** Don't be snobby about it—if you qualify, it's there for you. Each state has different Medicaid qualifications, so make sure to check with your state health department or go to **cms.hhs.gov,** the web site for the **Centers for Medicare and Medicaid Services.** This is especially important if you need to be hospitalized—it can save you thousands in medical bills.

## EMERGENCY CARE

If you're very sick or in an accident and have to go to a hospital emergency room, any and every hospital ER is **required** to assess and treat you—especially if it's life threatening—**before** asking you how you're going to pay the bill. The people there can't refuse to treat you until they squeeze out of you how you're going to pay. But be clear: It must be an emergency, and you will eventually be asked that question. If you're going to the emergency room for antibiotics for a bad back, the hospital only has to assess you—not treat you—before asking how you're going to pay. In any case, if you're going in only to see a doctor for antibiotics or another non-life-or-limb-threatening condition, go to a clinic. It'll be cheaper!

And remember, you may leave the emergency room without a bill, but you'll eventually get one—and it will be a biggie. **The ER is not free.** Unless . . .

Seek out a public hospital that is called a **Hill-Burton hospital.** Not only are these hospitals required to take you in without insurance, but if you can't afford to pay, they may have to waive the bill. The Hill-Burton Act was put into effect more than fifty years ago. It requires that hospitals that accept money from the federal government offer charity care and other services to the community in return.

Of course, hospitals are notorious for overcharging patients for simple items such as tissues and soap, cloaking them in obscure names to deflect from the fact they're asking $54 for a box of "mucus removal devices." If you do end up needing to pay for your hospital care, make sure to ask for (or if you have to, **demand) an itemized bill.** Even if you have health insurance, you may end up having to pay for overages, and you should closely check every item that you're being charged for. Be ready to refute needless charges and/or talk with the hospital's billing department—nicely—fairly often. They cannot refuse you an itemized bill—every state requires it. And don't accept "miscellaneous" items or fees that seem too general to be clear. Call the billing department and demand an explanation of these items.

Also, don't worry: In addition to starting your road to recovery, you are not required to pay your hospital bill before you leave the hospital. As a matter of fact, if you're not covered by insurance and will need to pay for your hospital stay on your own, **don't pay any of it before you leave the hospital.** Tell them to send you a bill. That's your right.

## PILLS, TEETH, EYES, ETC.

As if you don't already have enough to worry about, there are your teeth, your mind, your eyes, and your prescriptions.

### HEAD

Of course your **mental health** is just as important as your physical health. Unfortunately, the government and insurance companies don't fully agree—yet. So in the meantime, the most coverage you'll probably get under an insurance plan is a visit to a psychiatrist for a prescription. But if what you more likely need is talk therapy, you'll have to make do with a discounted bill for an in-network therapist. At least what you pay can be taken out of an FSA or HSA and is tax-deductible.

For lower-priced therapy, you can also seek out **mental health clinics** that work on **sliding scales,** basing their fee on how much you can afford to pay. You also may want to look into your local colleges and universities. Many have clinical and social work programs that offer low-cost therapy. If you're a bit adventurous and it's not an emergency, you could also sign up to take part in a therapeutic study so you can get an initial assessment and even therapy for free.

## Teeth

Americans are known for the care of our teeth, but this is becoming less and less manageable. Dental care costs have been going up faster than medical costs, and only half of American workers have dental coverage. Hopefully this will soon change as evidence continues to show that dental health is a factor in other more serious health issues such as heart disease. Dental care is a cash business—almost half of all dental care is paid for directly by patients. It's pricey, but very important for more than your smile, so at least pay to get your teeth cleaned as often as you can afford it.

**Universities** and **dental schools** are great places for low-cost or no-cost dental care. The thought of a student giving you a root canal may make you queasy, but if you really have no alternative, it's much better than losing your tooth. Plus, it's not as scary as it sounds. Students are always well supervised, and you'll probably get a better cleaning than you'll get at most dentist offices since Ms. Future Dentist really wants that A. To find other low-cost dental care in your area, visit the web site of the National Institute of Dental and Craniofacial Research (NIDCR), **nidcr.nih.gov.**

## EYES
Your eyes need checkups, too. Some employers offer **vision plans** that cover checkups, diagnostic tests, and any emergency situations or treatments for eye disease. But you will pay out of pocket for contact lenses and glasses and any vision-correction surgery, though you may get a discount on these for being part of a group vision program.

If you aren't covered and need an eye checkup or new contact lenses, check out local optometrists and opticians for deals. They have the equipment for diagnosing eye problems such as glaucoma or corneal damage, not to mention fitting you for contacts and/or glasses, and usually offer lower prices or waive the cost of the examinations if you buy your lenses with them.

If you have a more serious eye problem that needs treatment but you're not covered by a vision plan, go to the **American Optometric Association's** web site—**aoanet.org**—to locate low-cost or no-cost options near you.

## PRESCRIPTIONS
And finally, a hotbed of political banter, your prescriptions. The cost of prescribed medication in this country is amazing. We're the only leading country that doesn't impose price controls on

prescriptions, so our drug costs are astronomical. I'll refrain from a political rant here, but basically, when it comes to prescriptions, we're very screwed. Several years ago, I practically bought a whole pharmacy supply in Mexico City when I found that I could pick up my allergy prescription for about $50 less than what I paid out of pocket at home.

If you don't have prescription coverage under your individual or employment health insurance, short of charging your drugs on your credit card, you have a couple of resources. You can **ask your doctor for samples.** Doctors have closets full of drug samples. It doesn't hurt to ask if they can give you some—explain your financial situation and next time you may not even have to ask. And when you get a prescription filled at the pharmacy, make sure to **ask for generic** so at least you'll be paying the lowest price they have available.

The big thing now of course is ordering prescriptions online—mostly from pharmacies based in **Canada,** where drug costs are much lower. However, this is not legal in most states, and you cannot be completely sure that these drugs match in quality and safety the drug originally prescribed. The same goes for crossing the border to **Mexico**—you can't be sure what you're getting and you must have a doctor's prescription to bring the meds back across the border. Either is a risk.

Instead, on the web you can shop smart and find cost-comparison sites that give price quotes for FDA-approved medications—go to **PillBot.com, TogetherRx.com,** or **DestinationRx.com.**

In the meantime, we can hope and vote that drug costs will go down so not only the wealthy or insured breathe easy when picking up their prescriptions.

## LIFE INSURANCE AND DISABILITY COVERAGE

One kind of insurance that most adults have but you may not need yet is life insurance. Life insurance is **insurance for your survivors:** children, spouse, and anyone else you help take care of. If you're single, unmarried, and have no children, you don't need life insurance. Your debts will be forgiven when and if you pass away, so unless you are financially responsible for your grandmother, a sick uncle, or an aging parent, you don't need to pay for this kind of coverage.

If you live with a partner, or other family member though, you may want to get life insurance to help him or her afford to keep your home should you pass away. The choice is up to you, but if you do buy a life insurance policy, make sure it's clear who the beneficiaries are. When you're married, your spouse, and child or children, are the automatic and legal beneficiaries. But in the case of a domestic partnership, you'll need to make the benefit designation firm, in writing and in the policy.

Life insurance is a pretty common benefit for full-time workers, with 51 percent of employers offering the coverage according to the BLS's 2004 employee benefits report. If your employer offers it, enroll. The cost to you is very small, especially compared with health insurance premiums.

However, if you have a child or children and your employer doesn't offer life insurance coverage, run, don't walk, to your computer and start life insurance shopping. Your life insurance will help take care of your child(ren) if something happens to you.

When shopping for life insurance, **be very careful.** Life insurance is sold primarily by agents who have a commission-based impetus to push expensive policies on you. **Stay away from whole life policies.** This type of policy acts as an investment as well as insurance, but it's terribly expensive. And besides, life insurance is *not* the way to invest your money (see the next chapter for much better investment options). You can flat out say no to any agent who pushes whole life insurance on you.

Instead, you should be shopping for **term policies.** This is pure, basic life insurance, and as the name suggests it lasts for a certain term. You choose how long the policy will be in effect. There are many places on the web to compare prices (such as **IntelliQuote.com**), so feel free to do your initial shopping around online, rather than calling agents directly. You'll narrow down what you want and not have to deal with a pushy agent from the start.

But you also need to know **how much** life insurance you should be getting. The amount of life insurance you need depends on such things as:

- Your age and health.
- How many people you are financially responsible for.
- If you have a mortgage.
- Your salary.
- The value of any other assets you might have (cash and investments).

For example, let's say that you're a newly married twenty-nine-year-old who just bought your first home together with your new spouse and your mortgage balance is around $270,000. You make $42,000 a year, have benefits through your employer, and hope to retire at sixty-five. Since you contribute almost 50 percent to household expenses, you want to make sure that your spouse is covered in case you pass away. With all these items in mind (and you don't have children yet), you'll probably need a life insurance policy of almost $1 million. Wow! Yes, sounds like a lot, but at today's rates, you can get covered for around $450 a year or $35 or $45 a month.

To get your own insurance estimate online, try the calculator at **//moneycentral.msn.com/insure/welcome.asp.** It will give you a fairly thorough idea of how much life insurance you should sign up for.

## DISABILITY INSURANCE

If you're single and financially independent, I cannot emphasize enough how important it is to get disability insurance, especially if it's offered to you at work. You have a much bigger chance of getting injured in an accident or being diagnosed with a debilitating illness than you do of dying.

I've seen it myself with a co-worker—it can be a freak accident or illness that puts you out of commission and unable to work for a long period of time. If you can't work, eventually you won't get paid. How to keep your home and independence? That's what disability insurance is for—it replaces the regular income you lose if you cannot work due to illness or injury.

Disability insurance is not workers' comp—you'll only get workers' comp if you get injured on the job. The other 128 hours a week that you're not at the office (figuring a 40-hour work-week) need to be covered, too.

If your employer offers disability, make sure to sign up—pronto. And get yourself covered for as much of your income as you can afford. I'm not talking 100 percent income replacement, but you probably could do well on 70 percent or a bit less if you had to.

It can be expensive to purchase individual disability insurance, but you can get quotes from online insurance sites (see end of this chapter) or bigger providers such as Hartford or Cigna. Also check out **ahip.org,** the site of the America's Health Insurance Plans, where you can find or request a hardcopy of *Guide to Disability Income Insurance.*

## RENTER'S AND HOMEOWNER'S INSURANCE: PROTECT WHAT YOU HAVE

So we've run through the taking-care-of-me-and-mine insurances. Now how about covering everything you own? Let me run another little anecdote by you:

One night, when I was living in my first solo apartment (or should I say, box) in Manhattan, I heard what sounded like a giant rainstorm. I peeked out my window—nope, no rain. I checked my bathroom, no running water. But as I walked closer to my front door, the sound got louder and louder until I was hearing what sounded like a raging waterfall. It was coming from the apartment across the hall. My poor neighbor was the recipient of the water from a burst pipe in his ceiling that proceeded to flood the apartment, destroy all his electronics, and damage all his furniture, not to mention papers, books, bedding . . . A few buckets and mop-ups later, I still didn't have the gumption to ask the poor guy if he had rental insurance (he didn't seem to be in a chatty mood). But what I did do the next day was call up and order some of my own.

Only about a quarter of renters have rental insurance, but considering how cheap and (fairly) uncomplicated it is, rental insurance should be a best seller. It's true that your landlord has insurance, but that insurance covers only the building structure—it covers *nothing* that's yours. So if you're robbed, flooded, or burned out, or if your luggage gets lost or stolen when you travel, without rental insurance, you'll be starting from scratch.

But no need—no need! **Rental insurance costs as little as $10 to $30 a month.**

Basic rental insurance covers your belongings should they be lost, stolen, or damaged—including your luggage when you travel. Your basic coverage will also include **liability.** This is to protect you in case someone is hurt in your home or on your rental property. You will also be covered if something of yours—or your actions or a guest's—damages your landlord's property.

That's a lot of coverage for a couple of bills a month.

Look to the biggest players (State Farm, Allstate, Hartford, and their ilk) for rental insurance quotes online, and be sure to check out comparison sites such as **InsWeb.com** and **Insure.com.** You can get a quote from the company that has your auto insurance—they'll likely give you a good deal since you'd be a "multiple" customer. Ask family and friends, too, to see how they like their insurance and agent—good personal recommendations can take all the guesswork out of this process.

When you're deciding what kind of policy you need, take into consideration how much you think it would cost to replace all your possessions and whether you want your policy based on **replacement cost** or **actual value.**

I'll take the guessing out of that and tell you that you that if you have a computer, stereo, good television, and other electronic

YOUR CREDIT SCORE

Here it is again:

• Insurance companies use
your credit score to
determine how likely you are
to file a claim.

• The better your credit score,
the lower the premium you
pay, and vice versa.

equipment or fairly pricey items, **you want replacement cost.** Actual value is what you own minus depreciation. So if you're looking to replace your $300 television that's four years old, your actual value will be close to nothing because the value of your television has depreciated so much over those few years. Replacement cost, on the other hand, is the full amount of what it would cost to replace what you own. So if that television was a twenty-eight-inch Sony, you'll get from your insurance what it costs now to replace that make and model of television. Good deal and well worth the extra in monthly premiums.

As with health insurance, you'll have a **deductible**—what you cover on your own before your insurance kicks in. The higher your deductible, the lower your monthly premiums will be. So if you can swing an annual deductible closer to $500 or $800, you can cut your monthly premium by a third or more. But you don't want a deductible that's too high—the point here is to lessen financial strain. Make sure you can afford the deductible you choose.

Also be sure to consider the following when choosing rental or homeowner's insurance:

• What is the **per-incident limit on liability coverage**? Make sure it's high enough, and ask for more if it's not. It won't raise your premium by much.
• Do you have any very expensive items such as an engagement ring or heirloom worth more than $1,000? If so, get

a **rider** or **floater** policy as well. This is a separate policy to cover the more expensive items you own. And get a formal appraisal done on the value of the item so you can be sure to have the

Tip:
When insurance shopping, ask the rep about the company's turnaround time for claims.
**The faster the turnaround, the better the service.**

backup paperwork to warrant the claim, should you need it.

- Do you live in an area prone to earthquakes, floods, hurricanes, and tornadoes? If so, you're probably not covered for any of these under a basic policy. Get what's called an **endorsement** to cover you in case you're hit by any of these "acts of God." Again, a bit extra out of your pocket, but for most Americans a necessity.

- What is the **loss of use** coverage? If something happens that makes your home unlivable, you'll want your insurance to cover the cost of living someplace else while you fix up your home or find a new one.

- Do you work from a home office? If so, you may need to purchase a **home business rider** to cover the additional value.

- Be truthful about owning a **dog** or other animal. If your dog bites or injures someone, you want to make sure your liability coverage is set up to deal with a lawsuit.

Once you have an insurance policy (or anytime beforehand), you have one more very important chore to complete: **Take inventory** of all your belongings. There are various ways to do this. You can film a video of your home, opening closets and making sure that all of your belongings have made it on record. Then store the video along with a written or printed list of your

**Do you have a smoke detector?**

**CO$_2$ detector?**

**Sprinkler system?**

**Deadbolt on your front door?**

If so, make sure to **tell your agent** when putting together your policy. **These safety items can bring down the cost of your monthly premiums.**

belongings and their values (group things such as your clothing together and estimate replacement values) in a fireproof safe or safe-deposit box at your bank. You can also take photographs instead, attaching a list of values. To have even more backup, save your receipts from your purchases, bundle them together, and stash them in a fireproof safe or safe-deposit box at your bank. Your inventory and receipts are incredibly important and worthwhile if you have to file a claim.

**Homeowner's insurance** is very similar to rental insurance in terms of deductibles, inventories, riders, and endorsements. But unlike rental insurance, it's **mandatory** in most states.

Because you actually own the full structure of your home (or condo), your insurance will be higher than when you rented because your replacement cost coverage includes **rebuilding your home.** Make sure you get **100 percent** replacement cost coverage—it's the norm with homeowner's insurance to only insure 70 percent or so, but you'll want and need that full 100 percent when and if you ever have to rebuild.

Here are a few extra items to think about when getting homeowner's insurance:

- Similar to "loss of use" in rental insurance, **displacement coverage** covers the costs of your temporary living arrangements if your home is inhabitable.

- Liability coverage comes with a homeowner's policy, but it sometimes has a cap that's too low. Pay a bit extra to get **umbrella liability.**
- If you're in a home that's more than a few years old, an **ordinance coverage** rider will help cover any substantial costs that come up if you have to make improvements to bring your home up to new code.

If you have any substantial changes to what you own or your property one year, make sure to review your insurance policy and make any changes or additions needed.

Shit can and will happen, but if you're covered, you'll soon be right back on your financial feet.

## Web Links

**health.gov**  This government site for general health and insurance information has listings of government health agencies, clinics, and medical developments.

**cdc.gov** The site of the Centers for Disease Control and Prevention is your source for information on high-risk health insurance pools as well as info and stats on health and safety.

**fda.gov** The site of the U.S. Food and Drug Administration is another source for high-risk health insurance pools.

**healthinsuranceinfo.net**  A consumer source of info on health insurance, including types, rates, and sources.

**eHealthInsurance.com** A comparison site for health insurance quotes and general health insurance info.

**insWeb.com** Compare quotes and coverage for health, dental, disability, life, rental, and home insurance.

**insure.com** Visit here for advice and info on all types of insurance, plus links to purchase insurance policies online.

**intelliquote.com** A comparison site for life, health, and disability insurance.

**moneycentral.msn.com/insure** Get an idea how much life insurance you may need with this calculator.

**ahip.org** The site of American's Health Insurance Plans lets you find and request a hardcopy of the full *Guide to Disability Income Insurance.*

**dol.gov** The site of the U.S. Department of Labor. Click "Health Plans and Benefits" for info on COBRA, mental health benefits, and more.

**insurekids.com** Info on health insurance, hospitals, and medical coverage for kids, as well as general medical information.

**insurekidsnow.gov** Backed by the U.S. Department of Health and Human Services, this site lets you see if your child is eligible for low-cost health insurance.

**webmd.com** You'll find tons of medical and health info here, along with links to various medical journals, studies, health news and developments, and a symptom checker.

**mayoclinic.com** Health and medical information and news on staying healthy, the treatment and prevention of chronic diseases and other illness, and national health centers.

**medlineplus.gov** Look for current health news, results of clinical trials, and a directory of doctors, dentists, and hospitals.

**intelihealth.com** Medical and dental health information, plus a medication resource center.

**nccam.nih.gov** The site of National Center for Complementary and Alternative Medicine features info on alternative medicines and treatments, and tips on being a savvy health consumer.

**acog.org** The site of the American College of Obstetricians and Gynecologists. Find an ob-gyn or read newsletters and current ACOG news releases.

**freeclinic.net** The Free Clinic Foundation of America offers a national directory of free health and medical clinics.

**thehealthpages.com** Find doctors and review their ratings and disciplinary records, explore multiple health care options, and compare health insurance policies.

**//bphc.hrsa.gov** The site of U.S. Department of Health and Human Services and Bureau of Primary Health Care helps you find low-cost or no-cost health care.

**medkind.com** A free medical clinic resource.

**cms.hhs.gov** The Centers for Medicare and Medicaid Services's site will tell you if you qualify for Medicare coverage.

**nidcr.nih.gov** The site of National Institute of Dental and Craniofacial Research, can help you locate low-cost dental care in your area.

**aoanet.org** The site of the American Optometric Association, with low-cost or no-cost vision and eye care options where you live.

**pillbot.com** A price-comparison site for prescriptions (FDA-approved).

**togetherrx.com** Another price-comparison site for FDA-approved meds.

**destinationrx.com** Ditto.

CHAPTER

# 9

# The Magical 401(k)

### *And Other Ways to Multiply Your Money*

*"Visualize wealth and put yourself in the picture."*
—KRS One, Def Poetry Jam, 2004

"Invest money?! *What* money!"

Of course, it's impossible to invest if you're barely making your rent. And eating Cheerios every night so you can set aside a few dollars a week is not the answer (trust me, I've tried).

Or some of you are saying, "Puh-lease. I've been day trading online since I was seventeen." If this is you, skip this chapter— or wait, read on, because day trading may not be the best idea *juuust* yet.

You may feel like right now you're just scraping by. But at some point you're going to need to save some money and at one point, you're going to need to save *a lot* of money.

Saving money for **emergencies** or for when you're **out of a job** should be your first venture into the squirrel-hoarding-nuts-for-winter plan. But what other **goals** do you have? Ever plan on buying your next apartment or house? What about a down payment for a new car? How about your first nice long, quasi-fancy vacation with your new beau? Heck, even a sharp couch or sound system easily cracks a four-figure price tag. All of these things are good to save up for, rather than loading up on debt.

But what about **retirement**? Okay, maybe I'm dreaming that you're thinking about that now, or maybe it's just coming up seriously on your radar. But remember, it looks like by the time we retire (or want to retire), Social Security will either be gone or well reduced. And shoot, we'll probably end up having to manage our own Social Security anyway if it gets privatized.

And how long will we live? Well, in 1950, life expectancy was about sixty-eight years. If someone passes away from natural causes at that age these days, that's considered fairly young. In 2000, American life expectancy was seventy-seven years. Folks, we are living longer and longer, yet many of us still need and want to retire at some point.

So what do we do? Do we work until we're seventy (health willing) so we can have a good ten to fifteen years afterward on the golf course or by the pool? Or do we save harder, earlier, and more so we can kick off in our early sixties? I don't know about you, but working a bit longer certainly seems almost inescapable to me; at the same time, though, starting to save up now sounds pretty smart and self-satisfying.

Let's say you haven't become a parent yet (and for those who have, you know what I'm talking about). Why not set up automatic (so you don't even miss it) savings and investment plans now for some important goals before the hard-core savings plans for your offspring's schooling and college education creep up?

Give yourself a head start. As soon as you can start saving and investing, do so. Consider it your "Bill-to-Self."

First, though, unless you have a company-matched 401 (k) dangling in your face (more on that soon), there are a couple of tasks to nail down before you start setting aside some hard-earned cash to invest.

## First, Get Steady

It doesn't make any sense to save and invest if you've got high-interest debts to pay. That's not to say that you can't invest or save at all if you have debt.

Here's my little rule that will serve you well: **If you have high-interest debt—with an interest rate at or above 9 percent or 10 percent—pay the debt off first, before saving and investing.** If your debt has a lower interest rate—for example, if your student loan has a 5 percent rate—work the debt down but at the same time feel free to sock away some cash and invest where you can get a higher rate of return.

"How shocking!" some may say. Why save and invest when you have outstanding debts? Well, because the reality is that most young adults have student loans in the five figures, but with fairly low locked-in interest rates. Now, paying back a five-figure loan can take eons, but that low interest rate means that money you put away in savvy investments (and we're talking basic mutual funds here) can **earn a higher return than the interest you're paying out.** Therefore, you still make a profit.

If you wait too long to start putting away money for future goals such as a down payment on a home and retirement, you'll lose out big-time in **compound interest** and **dollar-cost aver-aging.** It's not worth waiting until you pay off that $43,000 student loan at a fixed 4.8 percent.

And what if you lose your job and have to live off credit for a while because you don't have any savings? Chances are that credit is going to have a much higher rate than your student loan. You need some savings.

So, first things first:

1. **Pay off high-interest debts.** Concentrate your financial energy on making those credit card or other high-interest loans disappear. Every month that you pay interest, you're losing money. And you *can* do this if you're committed. Go back to chapter 4 to learn how.

2. **Emergency cushion.** Before investing, put aside enough cash to cover you for **a minimum of three months**—six months if you have dependents—in case you're out of a job or another emergency limits your income. This peace of mind is worth a hundred times more than the dollar amount you have saved.

"Save? Ha!" you say. All right, you need every dollar, but what about if your savings account were set up as if it were a monthly or bi-weekly **bill**? Set yourself up with a savings account linked to your checking (where your pay is deposited) and have your bank automatically take out a set amount every two weeks or every month—like a bill. It may

To figure out how much you should have in your emergency stash, go to **dinkytown.net/savings.html** for an **emergency savings calculator.**

hurt a little in the beginning, but that one phone call or mouse-click that sets up your **automatic savings** in remembrance won't have hurt a bit, especially as you watch the account tick up and up and up. Actually, my best advice is **don't pay any attention.** Forget you have the account for a while—put it out of your mind so it can grow and you're not tempted to dip in here and there.

However, if you get a **raise** or new job with a higher salary, make sure to increase the amount going automatically into your savings. Even if it's only another $10 twice a month, you'll have a nice cushion in no time.

But is a savings account where your money should be after it builds up to a decent amount?

Good question. The answer is, probably not. I'll tell you the "why," but first, I'll arm you with the "how."

## THE WORKINGS BEHIND "GROWING" MONEY

When you put your money into an account or investment that earns interest, a very funky and marvelous thing happens over time: **The interest compounds.** You earn interest on your interest. This is a concept best illustrated by a potentially eye-crossing chart (following), but let me break it down for you.

Say you invest **$500** in an account that earns you an average **7 percent** interest every year. So, assuming you don't add to or subtract from that $500, after the first year you'll have **$535.** You continue to let it be, and the year after that you'll have **$572.45.** How? Because that 7 percent interest gets calculated on the original $500 the first year, but after that the 7 percent is calculated on the interest you've already earned as well. So coming into year two, that's 7 percent on top of your $500 and the $35 in year-one interest. Year two, the 7 percent is earned on top of that, and year three you'll have earned around $40 of interest for a total of **$612.52.** And so on, and so on.

Not only is your original $500 growing in interest every year, but **the interest you're earning earns interest**—voilà! That's compound interest, folks, and it's a wonder.

Just check out the crazy skew in the chart below to see how leaving money in an interest-bearing account can grow like a weed:

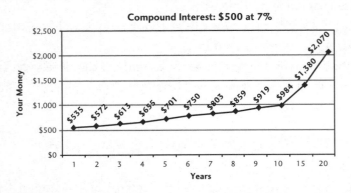

Compound Interest: $500 at 7%

So you'll have **doubled** your initial investment of $500 in around ten years, and you'll have **quadrupled** it in twenty. And all you had to do was set up the initial account.

However, you can do more—much more—to multiply your money. What would happen if you not only invested $500 at 7 percent, but every year **added another $500**? This amazing money-multiplying strategy is called **dollar-cost averaging.** It's really a complicated name for a simple thing—investing a set amount at regular intervals over time—but what its wack name refers to is the phenomenon of averaging the cost of your investment purchases over time.

I'll say that again: When you invest in something—say, a mutual fund—you're buying shares in that investment. So if you have $500, you can buy fifty shares at $10 each. But investments fluctuate. So one month you can buy fifty shares with your $500, but a year from now, another $500 will only buy you forty-two shares. But two years after that, your next $500 will buy you fifty-eight shares. By consistently investing a set amount at regular points in time, such as every year or month, you average out market fluctuations.

So when your investment shares go up, you can't buy as many shares as when the price was cheaper, but over time it averages out.

Okay, a bit too eggheaded maybe, but the point is that by putting your investments and savings on **autopilot,** not only will you reap the benefits of compound interest, but your investments will grow exponentially over time and rub out heavy losses along the way.

This one looks much better in a graph as well—here's your $500 at 7 percent, but instead of letting it just sit there all by its lonesome, you add another $500 every year:

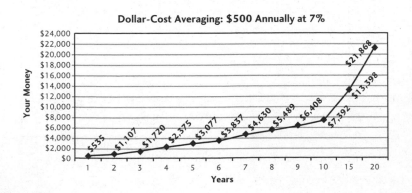

**Dollar-Cost Averaging: $500 Annually at 7%**

After investing $500 a year for ten years (for a total out of your pocket of $5,000) earning an average of 7 percent interest a year, you'll have around **$7,392.** That's a gain of **$2,392**—not bad! But even better, if you keep it up, in twenty years you'll have doubled your total investment of $10,000 to **$21,868.**

Let's say you're twenty-four years old now and you want to retire at sixty-two. Keep up that automatic annual $500 in the same account (which should be one of several investment accounts) and by the time you retire, you'll have **$98,860.** That's the sum from a total investment of **$19,500** out of your piggybank, plus **$27,265** of earned interest on that amount, plus **$52,095** (!) in compound interest. Good times.

Here's another scenario: What if you got to a point where you could have $50 every paycheck (every two weeks) automatically invested in a stock mutual fund, for example, that averages 8 percent interest? What would happen to that "Bill-to-Self" of $100 a month over time?

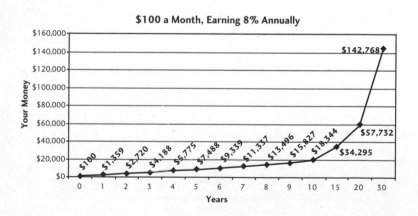

**$100 a Month, Earning 8% Annually**

Wow. So assuming that you don't raise the amount you invest—though if you can, of course you should—your investment of $100 a month over thirty years, earning an average of 8 percent a year, would net you **$142,768.** And that's from only $36,100 out of your pocket over thirty years. Just keep watering it and watch it grow.

There's another li'l math ditty that's helpful to know when you're trying to calculate how much you should invest and how it will grow: **the Rule of 72.** With this rule, the question is: **How long will it take for my investment to double?**

Simple. Say you have $1,000 to invest and you've found a nice spot for it that earns 8 percent interest annually. Seventy-two is the magical divider—how many times does your interest rate go into 72? Eight goes into 72 nine times. So it will take **nine years** for you to double your initial investment of $1,000. And it will double **every nine years.**

Here's another one: You have $1,000 at only **5 percent** interest. It will take you **14.4** years to double your investment. But if you can get a nice juicy **10 percent** annually for your $1,000, you'll have around $2,000 in **7.2** years.

### The Enemies of Money Multiplying

Oh, but there are wolves in the moneymaking forest, just waiting for a chunk of your spoils. So if you're investing—amen, rather than shoving your money in a box in the freezer—there are a few nasty truisms of life that can put a chink in your earning armor:

**Inflation • Taxes • Fees**

The good news is, if you save and invest smartly, you can either bypass some of these totally or make sure they get as little from you as possible.

## INFLATION

Do you remember when you were a kid and a gallon of milk cost around $1.59? Or maybe when you could buy a new album or tape for under $8? And a cup of coffee could be had for pocket change?

This sad tale of rising prices is called inflation, and we want our long-term savings and investments to outpace it over time. Inflation can sometimes plow ahead at a breakneck pace—such as in the early 1980s, when prices on most goods and services went up an average of 14 percent a year. But lately, inflation has been averaging about **2 to 3 percent** a year.

This is why it's never a good idea to stash large amounts of cash around as a savings measure (you hear that, Nana?)—it's going to be worth anywhere from **2 to 6 percent less** (or more) every year it sits there. Compound interest works backward too, you know. Even $100 in cash over twenty years loses tremendous value. Make sure to save and invest your money for longer-term goals in accounts that outpace inflation.

## TAXES

Death and taxes. Inevitable. As if a minus 3 percent on your money every year due to inflation weren't enough, you have to worry about taxes taking another lump out of your well-invested booty.

If you earn money—in savings and investments, called **gains**—you're going to have to pay taxes on it at one point or another.

That's another 23 or 38 percent chunk of your dough. If you can't avoid it, what can you do?

You can choose wise **tax-deferred** investments (to be discussed soon) that hold off on the tax munch until you retire. If you have other investments, make sure you know what the tax rate will be on any gains. Your goal here is to offset that amount by either increasing your investment or finding more tax deductions and credits.

### FEES

Of course, nothing's for free in the world of money, so you're probably going to get hit up for fees at some point when you invest. The fees on many savings accounts that pay interest can be bypassed by keeping all your accounts with one bank and linking them so your total meets the required no-fee minimum.

You can also shop around for the bank or company with the lowest fees on its savings and investment accounts. **More on fees later,** but make sure you read the fine print on any savings and investment agreement to see where and how fees are assessed. Up front? Monthly? Annually? A onetime processing fee, or a fee-per-transaction?

## THE MAGICAL 401 (K) AND OTHER TAX-FRIENDLY PLANS

Before I even get into the basics of investing—*what's a stock, bond, mutual fund . . . ?*—there is one investing tool that is so important that if it's available to you, you should run down to your benefits office to sign up. That would be the 401 (k).

And if you aren't offered a 401 (k) at your job, you have

other tax-happy investment options that I'll review for you as well.

These are just too good (because of the tax savings) for you to wait.

Back in the day, when there were such things as company loyalty and company "men," there was also a thing called a **pension.** A pension was a savings fund your company set up for you, in addition to your salary, so that once you were ready to retire— after slogging away there for twenty-five or so years—you could still take home anywhere from 50 to 80 percent of your salary. Add Social Security to that, and you're livin' large in your old age.

However, the pension is going the way of VHS. Nowadays, the piddly 20 percent or so of Americans who still get a pension— usually government and public workers such as firefighters and cops—take home only 21 percent of their retirement income from their pensions.

What is there to take the place of pensions?

Not perfect, but better than nothing, up pops the **401 (k).**

While trying to find a way to minimize the tax bite for some fat cats in the late 1970s, banker Ted Benna clasped his hands and asked for a better inspiration than those rich jokers. The answer he got (and yes, he believes it was divine inspiration) was taking advantage of a congressional tax-code loophole that gave American workers a lawful right to save and invest a percentage of their pre-tax income. Named after Section 401, paragraph (k) of the U.S. tax code, Ted Benna's big idea caught on tight in the late 1980s. Now there is more than $2 trillion (that's with a *t*) held in 401 (k)s, about 40 percent of total private retirement savings in the United States.

Brilliant. We love lawful loopholes to keep our tax bites down. But what exactly are 401 (k)s and how do they work?

The 401 (k) is an **employee retirement savings and investing plan** that allows full-time employees of participating employers to set aside anywhere from 1 to 6 percent of their pre-tax income into an investment account. There are maximums in how much you can invest—some 401 (k)s allow 9 percent or more—in one year, depending on your income. The maximum percentages you're allowed to contribute each year are set up according to the maximum amount allowed by the government each year to put aside tax-free.

In 2004, the maximum you could contribute to your 401 (k) tax-free was $13,000. For **2005,** that number went up to **$14,000.** The numbers will continue to rise with inflation. Also, if you're over fifty—because this is planned as a method of financing retirement—you get to add an additional $4,000 annually tax-free.

However, you have to pay taxes at some point. Your 401 (k) accumulates without taxes. That can be years and years of money piling up, earning interest and good returns, without taxes. That in and of itself is like getting a raise of 25 to 38 percent on what you're contributing to the plan. It's a good amount of "free" money. But **you pay taxes when you withdraw the money for retirement.** So starting up a 401 (k) as soon

If you **leave a job** where you have a 401 (k), make sure to **roll it over** to a new plan—either your new employer's, or your own—and **check your contribution percent.**

Sometimes the amount of your contribution rolls over automatically, and other times you're enrolled at a different amount.

**You don't want to lose what you've built up, or lose out on more.**

as you can when you're young makes the most sense because you'll have so many years to accumulate funds in your account that the tax bite at the end will be a small percentage of what it could have been had you paid taxes in the first place. But if you're older and have only ten years or so to retirement, you don't have much time to take advantage of the tax-deferred benefit of the 401 (k). Your end-bite may be just as big as your during-bite.

There is another crazy cool component of many 401 (k)s— your company may **match your contribution.** Most companies that offer 401 (k)s also match a percentage of the contributions you make (all in lieu of a pension plan, usually), such as 50 percent of the first 5 percent you contribute. After a certain number of years with the company (your time **vested**), you are entitled to the full 100 percent of the company's match.

That's another chunk of free money! Okay, yes, it's an "employee benefit," but it's basically your employer saying, *Hey, save some money and I'll add to your stash the same amount you do.* That, my friends, is a tremendous benefit especially compared with other long-term savings options.

If you work for a nonprofit, your 401 (k) will be called a . . .

**403 (b)**

If you're at a government agency, your 401 (k) is called a . . .

**457**

And why do companies do this? Not from the goodness of their hearts, unfortunately. More so because traditional pension plans are too expensive. A 401 (k) costs a firm less than half as much as a standard pension.

So if your employer offers a 401 (k) match, you could potentially sock away $1,000 or much more every year—tax-free—and receive an additional $1,000 or more on top of that. That helps out, no doubt.

Enrollment in 401 (k) is usually offered to employees after a year at the company. If you have this opportunity, sign up pronto. And if you can only afford to contribute a small percentage— say, 1 percent or 2 percent—this year, go ahead anyway. Then when you get a raise, also raise what you're paying yourself in your 401 (k). Or every year, make it a point to bring up your contribution 1 percent until you clear the maximum allowed.

According to the ever-probing BLS, 59 percent of workers as of early 2004 have access to retirement benefits such as a 401 (k) from their employers. And of those with access, only 50 percent participate. Darn it.

Now, the 401 (k) has its critics—and it should. In the very ugly market crash and slump of the late 1990s, 401 (k)s took a huge hit. Why? **Because 401 (k)s are market investments.** It's a misnomer to call a 401 (k) a savings plan alone. It's not that benign. A 401 (k) places your money in investments—to grow and build, of course—but if you're not careful, your investments can go down, way down. And that's what they did for thousands and thousands of folks who were close to retirement. All their gains over the years were wiped out by a plunging stock market.

Which is why you need to actively manage your 401 (k), not just sign up and let it sit. When you start it up, you'll be assigned an account with someone such as

> Don't tap your 401 (k) to pay off debts or loans. Borrow against it only in an emergency. Otherwise you'll get creamed with taxes and penalties—from a quarter to half of your total savings. Also, if you borrow, you'll lose out on earnings if you can't pay the money back right away.

Fidelity, Schwab, or E*Trade, and you'll have to pick and choose where your money will be invested. In the next section, I'll review the basics of investing and give you a head start in figuring out where to put your stash. If you're young, you'll probably want some fast-growing investments that may be a tad risky, but you'll have more time to recover any losses than a fifty- or sixty-year-old.

There are two dangers in 401 (k)s:

- **Investing too much in company stock.** This is definitely a basic no-no. It's good to love the company you work for and have faith in its ability to grow and prosper, but there is no bigger mistake than putting your 401 (k) in the hands of company stock. If you want stock in your company, make it a smidgen—less than 10 percent. You need to **diversify** your investments to protect what you have—maximize earnings while minimizing losses over time.

- **Not paying attention to what your 401 (k) is invested in.** With a 401 (k), your company may be helping you by setting up the benefit and potentially matching your contributions, but after that you're on your own. You and only you are responsible for how the funds in your 401 (k) are invested. Get savvy on what is offered and where you want it to go. Take a peek at it every couple of months or so, and **reassess** where your money is from time to time—moving what needs to be moved or switching around the percentages you've allocated to each investment. If you don't like the investment options your employer has for you, see if there is an **opt-out** where you can choose to invest somewhere else without penalty.

All this will make much more sense to you after the following section, but be assured that 401 (k)s are not the beast that those burned several years ago may think. You certainly don't have to depend (nor should you) on your 401 (k) to be your sole investment, but if it's offered, it's a great one.

### Don't Have Access to a 401 (k)?

Thankfully there isn't only one way to save money while deferring taxes. You can put money every year into an **individual retirement account (IRA).** A traditional IRA lets you contribute up to **$4,000 a year** (for a single tax filer, as of 2005), and what you earn is tax-deferred until you withdraw it. Also, whatever you invest in an IRA each year—up to the max amount allowed—may be **tax-deductible** as well. That's a nice one–two tax break.

Many investment firms manage IRAs, such as **Schwab** and **Fidelity,** but you can also start one up where you do your regular banking and possibly cut down a bit on fees.

An IRA, just like a 401 (k), is a great retirement or long-term investment tool since the tax bite waits until the money is withdrawn (at or after fifty-nine and a half years of age). But again, you have to choose where the money gets invested and make sure not to withdraw early, subjecting you to mega fees, penalties, and an extra 10 percent tax slap.

An IRA is available for anyone under the age of seventy and a half who earns a living, no matter how much or how little. In contrast, a **Roth IRA** is specifically set up for folks who earn **below $110,000** as a single or **$160,000** married, filing jointly.

> You can have both an IRA and a 401 (k), but you may not qualify for a tax deduction.

There are circumstances when you can withdraw funds from your IRA or Roth IRA *without* incurring any penalties or the 10 percent early-withdrawal tax penalty:

- A first-time home purchase (up to $10,000).
- If you become disabled and unable to work.
- Medical expenses that add up to more than 7.3 percent of your income.
- Qualified higher education expenses.

The big difference here is that what you contribute comes from after-tax income and is **not tax-deductible.** However, you can withdraw from this account at any time, without any penalties. You don't have to be fifty-nine and a half to start taking money out, and you won't pay any extra for doing so, though if you take money out before the account's **fifth** anniversary, you may be subject to federal taxes and a 10 percent tax penalty.

Because it doesn't have a time limit per se and is therefore not so much a retirement plan as a general investment plan, a Roth IRA is a good tool for various long-term investments such as a child's college education or a down payment for a second home.

If you're **self-employed** but are lucky enough to be a boss and have employees who work for you, your tax-deductible savings and investing tool is called a **Keogh.** This is a retirement account that allows you to contribute a percentage of your income **pre-tax,** up to an annual max.

Even if you work **part-time,** you get your own pre-tax, tax-deferred plan, called a **SEP-IRA (simplified employee pension IRA).** Just like a Keogh, you contribute a percentage of your pre-tax income every year—which, depending on how much you're making, is also tax-deductible.

## INVESTING BASICS:
## DIVERSIFICATION AND THE MARKETS

Okay, so you're on the up-and-up with tax-friendly investments and their annual maximums, and want (and need) to make some returns in different investments. What if you have only $50 to start? Or suppose you suddenly get an inheritance of several thousand dollars?

You have plenty of options, so I'll give you an overview of the basics so you can make informed decisions on where you put your money. Because one of the most important concepts in investing is knowing the game: the where, how, and when. It never makes sense to buy anything you don't understand.

### Start Building

Say you have a small amount to start investing, but don't want your money sitting in your checking account available for a late-night ATM withdrawal as well as failing to earn any interest or return—but, you're also not ready to run the risks of the stock market. These days, you have plenty of options.

If you want an alternative to your basic savings account, you have several popular short-term, low-risk choices. Unfortunately, though, because interest rates are very low right now, these places to sock away money are not as attractive return-wise as they have been in the past. Still, you'll be earning something and you won't have to worry about losing your money in a market crash or company scandal:

- **High-yield savings accounts** earn a tad higher interest for you while still keeping your money available for withdrawals or transfers (keeping it **liquid**). Regular savings accounts can have interest rates as low as .45 percent (chicken feed), while high-yield savings can reap you at least .75 percent. For example, there's Chase's select rate of 1.69 percent and ING's Orange Savings, which currently offers 2.35 percent. But with these accounts, make sure to read the fine print on minimums and any fees that can wipe out interest earnings.

- **Money market accounts** offer interest rates similar to high-yield savings accounts, but the interest rates go up as you bypass certain dollar amounts. The higher your account balance, the higher your earnings.

- **Certificates of deposit (CDs)** are banking products that you buy and own for a certain period of time—a term. The longer the term on your CD, the higher your interest rate and earnings. So a **six-month CD** will get you **1.7 percent** in interest, but if you can commit to fifteen months instead, you'll see something closer to 2.75 percent—and for **five years** you're looking at **3.6 percent.** But be careful about needing to withdraw your CD before its term is up. You can end up saying bye-bye to three to six months' interest earnings as a penalty. And note that CDs tend to renew automatically, so keep track of the maturity date of what you buy. You'll have a **grace period of seven to ten days** to decide to cash out or roll it over for another term.

## DIVERSITY AIN'T JUST FOR THE WORKPLACE

When it comes to alternatives to basic, safe, lower-earning savings accounts and CDs, you have more access to good investments now than any other time in history. Not only rich guys play the markets these days. What's best about it is that with mutual funds and index funds, anyone with $1,000 or more can get fairly safely into the stock and bond market—earning very good returns—without spending the time researching and gambling on individual stocks and bonds. There are a lot of chances to lose money in bad investments or get hit with ridiculous fees, but if you're smart there's a cornucopia of investment options out there.

However, there are two very important concepts to review before we get to investing: asset allocation and diversification.

Your investments are called **assets.** And the practice of where you put your investments is called **asset allocation.** It's a tad more complicated than it sounds, though. Depending on how old you are, how much money you have, and how far away—or close—your investment goal timetable is, your asset allocation will and should differ.

For example, say your parents got hit badly by the internet bust, but they only have another ten years or so until retirement. Do they invest their money into high-return but high-risk investments to recoup the losses they sustained several years ago? Or do they remix their portfolio to adjust their asset allocation to maximize growth but keep risk minimal since they don't have time to make up for any more big losses? The answer would be the latter—a **conservative** asset allocation.

But if you're twenty-seven years old and are saving for retirement, you have lots of time to buy-and-hold your investments, knocking out losses with a combination of time and investing more and more every year (dollar-cost averaging, yes?). You can sustain—and should take—more risk than your parents. Your asset allocation can be **aggressive,** with a full 85 percent in stocks (various kinds and funds, of course) and the rest in more conservative investments such as bonds.

When you get older and closer to the date you need the money, your investments need to be weighted so you're exposed to less risk. When you're younger, you have more time and can afford more risk. As your life changes—you get married, want to buy a house, have children, and save for their college—you adjust your asset allocation.

For example: Dave is twenty-seven years old. After five years of toiling in the back office, he just got a great new job with full benefits and a 401 (k). But he has to choose where to allocate the money going into his 401 (k). What's the best mix for him?

Well, he's young and has at least another twenty to thirty years until retirement. He's engaged, the wedding is a year away, and they're not thinking of having children until a couple of years after that. Dave's not afraid of taking some risks with his investments as long as the returns might be better. And because he wants to buy their next home, he wants to sock away as much as he can now to use some funds penalty-free for the down payment.

Dave is ready for an **aggressive** asset mix. He has many years ahead of him to ride out any substantial losses or market falls, and he has all the more to gain in returns over time. He can stand to put 85 to 90 percent of his assets into stocks and stock funds. Of that, he can divide up his holdings with somewhere around 20 percent in potentially high-earning but riskier foreign or global stocks and another 20 percent in small-cap stocks (more on this soon). The 10 percent to 15 percent of his assets not in stock-related investments can go into bonds, which are lower in returns but very stable.

However, when Dave gets around to having a family and owning a home, he may want to shift 10 percent out of stocks and into bonds to beef up the stability of his portfolio. And the closer he gets to retirement, the less he should

> You should never have more than 10 percent of your money in one stock.

have in stocks, because he'll need more stability and less risk.

To get an idea of what your percentages should be compared with say, your parents', visit *Money* magazine's "Fix Your Mix" calculator at **money.com/tools** (click "Asset Allocator").

Where you put your money should be based on **diversification.** If your investments are well diversified, you'll be protected from being demolished by huge and sudden losses. For example, in the late 1990s many folks (financial professionals included) got swept up by internet stocks and day trading—they were not well diversified. They focused on one type of stock, one or two types of industries, and put too much money into one kind of investment. This exposed many to horrible losses.

If your assets are diversified, you'll be better protected from losing a lot of money. So nope, you shouldn't be totally invested in bonds or in stocks, but rather in a nice, balanced mix.

### THE GOODS

Let's say you're ready to put a good chunk of money away **for at least three to five years** and you've got the stomach to handle a few ups and downs of the market. This is when you're ready to take your first dip into investing in the markets.

You hear the words all the time—*stock, bond, fund, Dow,* and so on. And you surely have an *idea* what they mean, but I'm going to give you a cut-and-dried review of these—and more—

investing basics. I'm not doing this to encourage you to get hooked on trading stocks or funds (not unless you have an extra ten hours a week to devote to hard-core research), but so that when it comes time for you to manage your 401 (k), or invest your first stack of bills, you know more about where you should put it and how changes in the markets or economy affect your investments.

## STOCKS

Investing in stocks holds the biggest risks for investors, but also provides the highest returns. If you're young and have a long investment horizon in front of you, investing in the stock market (or, better, stock mutual funds—more soon) is a very good idea. But you really need to know what you're doing, so here's the 411:

When you buy a stock, you are buying a piece of a company (because it takes money to build and run a business). You are putting your money into a business, hopefully because you believe in it, you **understand its business,** and you're planning that if the company does well, your investment will be worth more.

Some companies pay **dividends** to their stockholders (look for DIV next to the stock symbol when it's listed in the papers or online). Dividends are a company's way of sharing the wealth— not only do you make a profit if your stock in this company goes up, but the firm regularly pays earnings out to you and the other stockholders as well. Many financial pros believe that dividend-paying stocks are some of the most reliable around, because companies that pay dividends are much more likely to have high valuations, and have built up strong businesses with many assets.

When dealing with stocks and bonds, you'll hear about **yield.** Yield is the percentage of return (earnings) paid on your stock in annual dividends. It's your dividend expressed as a percentage rather than a dollars-per-share amount. If you're earning a $2 dividend per share, your yield is 2 percent.

**Stock markets,** including the NASDAQ, the AMEX (American Stock Exchange), the NYSE (New York Stock Exchange), state stock markets such as the Philadelphia Exchange or the Chicago Exchange, and even electronic exchanges like Archipelago, are the places where stocks are traded.

Stock prices rise and fall on these trading floors in tandem with how well their business is doing (and sometimes, prices are inflated because people believe too much hype—see internet stocks in 1998 and 1999). For example, So-and-So & Co. just reported that it made more money this quarter (the calendar year is broken up in quarters for business reports) than it expected, so its stock goes up that day because it did well. And it'll be expected to continue to do well in the near future. Not only is the company worth a bit more on the accounting books, but your stock price/value goes up because people feel that having a piece of the company is worth more. Of course, the opposite happens when a company does badly or—as in the case of Enron—when the shit hits the fan and the public finds out that the big cheeses were lyin', cheatin', and stealin'.

How do you decide what's a good business (or stock) to invest in? Well, unless you have several thousand dollars and can afford to lose a big chunk of it, individual stock picking is a very difficult and very risky thing to do. (You should never, ever put more than 10 percent of your money into an individual stock—invest only what you're prepared to lose.)

But it's always good to know the language with which the stock wonks speak:

**P/E** This refers to a stock's **price-to-earnings ratio.** It's a number that gives you a hint as to how a stock is doing— whether it's overhyped or undervalued, for example. The P/E is the stock's **price divided by the profits** (per share) the company made in the past year. So if the company isn't doing well and had losses, but the price of its stock is high, you'll have a very high P/E and the stock is a risk. A 15 to 20 P/E is stable and good, but P/Es don't just stand alone— you have to compare a stock's P/E with those of other stocks in the same industry to see if this is a normal or middle P/E for the industry, or if your particular stock is skewed. Also, a high P/E may be a good thing—is the company projected to do very well because of an upcoming deal or legal finding? Complicated, yes, but good to be familiar with.

**Market caps** When you hear about small-cap, large-cap, or mid-cap stocks, the shorthand is standing in for levels of "market capitalization." Market cap refers to the stock market value of a company, calculated by multiplying the current share price of a stock by the number of shares on the market. So a **small-cap** stock refers to a company whose stock market value is less than $1.5 billion, a **mid-cap** stock is pegged at a valuation between $1.5 billion and $10 billion, and a **large-cap** stock refers to the big kahunas with a market value of better than $10 billion.

**Blue chips** These are the "old school" companies of the stock exchange, such as IBM. The stock of these companies is usually the least risky on the market—they've been around for a very, very long time, and have high and solid values.

**IPO (initial public offering)**  This refers to the first time a company ever issues stock, allowing investors to begin to invest in its business. Google in 2004—wow!—is a prime example of a hot IPO. This search engine company offered its first stock with an opening price of around $95; in less than three months, that price had risen to a very high $195. Most IPOs are quite a bit less exuberant.

**Growth, value, and income stocks**  Stocks are popularly lumped into different groups considered appropriate for various investment styles based on volatility, earnings, potentials, and dividends. A **growth stock** is one with high earnings and lots of potential for income, but also a lot of risk. A **value stock** is one with a depressed P/E or value because something happened to the business, but it's ready to come back strong. And **income stocks** are steady and strong, earning high dividends and creating steady income.

**The Dow**  This is shorthand for "the Dow Jones Industrial Average"—a measure of how the stock market, in general, is doing that day. The Dow compiles the stock prices of thirty longtime industrial behemoths (such as Coca-Cola) and shows how much their prices go up and down each day. Market measures like the Dow used to be expressed in dollar amounts (which is what they are), but now they are spoken of and listed as **points** with percentages—say, "the Dow went up forty and a half points today." Other stock market barometers include the **S&P 500** (Standard & Poor's five hundred handpicked stocks) and the **NASDAQ,** a market that focuses on "new" economy companies and industries, such as tech.

## BONDS

Bonds tend to be a more conservative investment, and since you're young, they shouldn't make up a lot of your portfolio. Still, it's good to understand the market. Also, eventually you'll probably want to make bonds part of your investing portfolio. So here's the lowdown on the world of bonds.

When you buy a bond, you are lending a company or the government (local, national, state) money for its business. Then it pays you **interest** on the money it's borrowing from you (called a **coupon**) and promises to pay it back in a certain amount of time. Bonds are issued and available for sale for a particular term, so when the bond **matures,** it's time to repay your money. If you want to pull your money out of a bond before it matures, you'll pay penalties that may wipe out your interest profits.

The interest rates available on bonds follow closely the **interest rate set by the Federal Reserve.** As I write, federal interest rates are at an all-time low, but bond investors are expecting them to go up. Bond prices run inversely to interest rates: When interest rates go up, it's a not a good time for bond owners and sellers. When interest rates rise, bond prices go down and vice versa.

> Bonds with terms of three to seven years historically have gains of 80 percent or more and 50 percent less risk than bonds with longer terms.
>
> —*Money,* 2004

There is some quirky vocabulary in the bond world, including **par value,** which refers to the price of the bond at the time you buy it. And unlike stocks, because bonds are offered for set time periods and pay out a fixed schedule of interest payments, they're called **fixed-income investments.**

Though bonds may seem like a dull, set-in-stone investment, their prices and interest rates fluctuate, making them more or less attractive for investors. A bond can be worth more than the face value it was issued at. If it sells at this higher price, it trades at a **premium.** If a bond is sold for a lower price than its face value, it's sold at a **discount** (that's an easy one). If the face value of a bond equals its market value, it's sold at **par.**

Here are more funky, but common, bonds terms:

**T-bills**  These are treasury bills—short-term bonds issued by the U.S. Treasury. They are issued in very short terms of thirteen weeks, twenty-six weeks, and one year (bonds are usually issued from five- to thirty-year terms). These sometimes fast earners are sold at a discount, and when they mature, they go back to you at par—the difference between the discount and the par value is your profit. The only time you'll get near these is if you have at least $10,000 to buy one, or if you own a fund that invests in them.

**Munis**  Shorthand for "municipal bonds," these large investments are bonds issued by local and state governments to raise funds for local and state projects. You can't get into them unless you've got at least $5,000 or are investing through a fund. The cool thing about these bad boys is that your interest earnings are free from not only federal taxes, but also state and local if you live in the locale you're investing in.

**Credit risk** Hey-hey, we're not the only ones who are judged on our creditworthiness and credit rating. Bonds—since they are borrowing money from their investors—need to have good credit ratings, too. A bond's credit risk refers to the chance that the bond issuer won't be able to pay back the money it's borrowed in the form of bonds. You can check out bond credit ratings with **Standard & Poor's** or **Moody's.** Just like high school, A's are great but anything lower than a B is a no-no.

## MUTUAL FUNDS

In order to be well diversified in stocks or bonds, you'd have to have $50,000 or more to spread around in a healthy way yourself. And for the rest of us? No problem: Mutual funds are an awesome way to invest in the markets without having to rely on your own company-earnings-report-reading-and-analysis abilities (yuck). Funds also offer you loads of choices depending on your goals, risk tolerance, and investing style. Another advantage is that there are fund companies that are willing to get you started with **as little as $100** as long as you set up an automatic, regular deposit plan. So let's break it down.

Mutual funds are managed groups of stocks or bonds (or a mix of both) and are a great investing tool. It takes a lot of hard work to research companies in depth, review their earnings statements, and pull together a group of investments that suit your needs. If that's too much for you, however, the folks who run mutual funds do it for you—grouping investments into funds that serve different investing needs and offer various levels of risk. When you invest in a mutual fund, you become a partial owner of a portfolio of investments.

There are as many different kinds of mutual funds as there are stars in the sky (or at least it feels that way). Actually, there are about five thousand stock funds around today. So how the heck are you supposed to choose? Well, take several things into consideration:

- How much do you need to invest?
- What do they invest in—stocks? Bonds? Growth industries?
- What's the risk level—high? Low? Mid?
- What is the history of return? How consistent—or not—is it?
- Are there many fees—processing fees, entry fees, commissions?

The biggest fee you can come across when investing in mutual funds is commission, which is called a **load.** Of course, as a beginning investor it's wise for you to search out **no-load** or low-load funds. About **a third of mutual funds are no-load,** and you can find them at **discount brokers** such as Charles Schwab or Fidelity. Whether a fund has a load or not doesn't tell you much about its quality as an investment. Loads are better indicators of levels of service. When you have a very large amount of money to invest, you may turn to funds with loads because the commission isn't that expensive given your overall portfolio and you may need more hand-holding at that point. In the meantime, you'll do just fine with no-load funds.

And when it comes to expenses, fund tables will show you expenses as a percentage of assets. You want a fund that is **at or under 1 percent.**

> **DECIPHERING MUTUAL FUND TABLES**
>
> **NAV**
> The price of one share of the fund.
>
> **NET CHG**
> How much a fund share lost or gained from the previous day.
>
> **YTD%RET**
> The year-to-date (since January 1) return on the fund—profit in a percentage.

To find information on mutual funds and which have the best records and lowest loads and fees, check out magazines, newspapers, and web sites that have annual mutual fund rankings such as *Money, Business Week,* and *The Wall Street Journal.*

For online guidance, though, **Morningstar.com** is the authority and has piles of fund information and star-based rankings (**four and five stars are awesome**). But the best part of using this site is its fund screening capabilities. Say you have a certain amount to invest, you don't want to pay a load, and you're a moderate-risk investor. Select your preferences and needs and you'll get a list of funds that are best for you. Morningstar also groups funds and compares them with other funds at their level. So if you want to see how a large-growth fund has done against other large-growth funds, the site shows you a comparison of performance records.

Know this, though: Mutual funds are run by people (managers, actually), so they are subject to the faults and strengths of people as well. You might find a couple of funds that invest in similar products, but differ widely in performance—lots of that has to do with how they're managed, or **investment style.** Just like individual stocks, you can look for funds that are **small-cap, mid-cap, growth, value,** what have you. So make sure to do some comparison shopping and match up your mutual fund investments with your **asset allocation pie** (what percentage of your money goes into high-growth high-risk, what goes into more conservative investments, and so on).

> Buying and holding an index fund can get you an average of 10 percent annual return. Cool.

There is one type of mutual fund with a fairly consistent track record of earnings and low fees—the **index fund.** Index funds are portfolios that group together and then follow all the stocks tracked in certain indexes, such as the **S&P 500.** For example, if you buy shares in an S&P 500 index fund, your investment goes up and down at closely the same rate as the S&P 500—the index in which you're investing. But, like any investment in the stock market, no matter how well diversified, there are going to be some index funds that do better than others, depending on when you invest. For example, an index fund that follows the tech market may not do as well as one that follows pharmaceuticals. Or an index fund that follows auto manufacturers' stocks right now may not do as well as one that follows real estate company stocks. But five or ten years from now, things may be vice versa.

As long as you're well informed, investing in index funds can be an amazing thing—although, because they are not the most risky type of investment, they are not the highest earning. They are consistent earners over long periods of time, however, and you can be assured that if you hold on to your index fund (a **buy-and-hold** strategy is a good one) you'll average the same return as the market you're following, averaged over time. If you're looking at the S&P 500, you will have beaten the earnings of over 85 percent of other funds in the past couple of years. Not bad.

## TYPES OF FUNDS

**Money market funds (aka money funds)** Fairly liquid low-risk, low-return short-term investments built with products such as CDs or T-bills. Good for short-term savings.

**Stock funds** Funds built from groups of stocks. Higher risk but much higher returns. Great long-term investment tool. Includes **international** stock funds (risky) and **sector** funds that cover certain types of industry.

**Index funds** Funds built on investments that match a particular index, such as the S&P. Lower risk than stock funds, good consistent returns, and low fees.

It's not just the fact that these funds (there are close to two hundred available) hold and follow big benchmark indexes that makes them a good spot for your money. It's because they're cheap—sometimes with expense ratios of less than .2 percent, compared with actively managed funds that run up to 1.5 percent or more. **Index funds have very low fees** because most of the work has been done for you. Fund companies don't have to pay a group of managers to manage an index fund. All the investments for the portfolios are chosen already, by the indexes. You can save a big chunk on your returns by not paying heavy fees, so index funds serve you two ways: winning returns over time and low fees.

The information in this chapter may seem a level above goobly-gook to you now, or maybe it's whetted your whistle to start making your money multiply (that's more what I was hoping for). Or maybe you knew all this stuff, but weren't sure how to apply it.

Whatever the case, I hope you've pulled out some savvy strategies for making your money grow—maybe not now, but definitely in the future. There is no excuse for not **paying your-self** and investing in yourself as soon as you're able.

As Chris Rock says, there is a difference between being **wealthy** and being **rich.** Wealth is built and maintained, while riches easily disappear. You may not want or need to be wealthy, but you certainly can take your piece of the American pie and set yourself up for lasting security, some short-term goals, and some more long ones. Ain't no one else gonna do it for you.

Happy investing.

## Web Links

**morningstar.com** This jam-packed info site has everything "markets," from stocks, bonds, mutual funds, and indexes to company news, investment ratings, and comparisons.

**fundalarm.com** An irreverent site with info on mutual fund activity, news, and management changes. Its motto is "Know when to hold 'em, know when to fold 'em."

**maxfunds.com** A "fun" mutual fund site (as fun as they can be) with info and Q&A on funds and fund news.

**401k.com** Fidelity's 401 (k) home page offers general 401 (k) info, retirement planning, and more.

**psca.org** The site of Profit Sharing/401 k Council of America, with info and resources on 401 (k)s and finding a service provider.

**citi.com** Citibank's site has full banking services; loads of info on funds, investing, savings, CDs, and bonds; top-ten stock lists; and market quotes.

**chase.com**  The site of Chase bank, with full banking and investment services, along with info on various savings accounts, CDs, bonds, stocks, and mutual funds.

**moneycentral.com**  This MSN and CNBC web site offers up-to-date info on investing and markets; investment and retirement calculators; indexes; and market activity, commentary, and analysis.

**money.cnn.com**  The site of *Money* magazine and CNN news. Look for info on financial planning, investing, market news, advice, and commentary.

**etrade.com**  Not just for day traders anymore, this online investing site offers info and options for other investments such as mutual funds and portfolio management.

**ameritrade.com**  Another online investing site, featuring info and investment options, plus comparisons of commission rates and fees.

**ingdirect.com**  The site of ING bank, with high-yield savings and other investment options.

**schwab.com**  Discount broker Charles Schwab's site has long-term savings and investing options, including 401 (k)s.

**fidelity.com**  The site of Fidelity Investments. You'll find investment products, advice, low-cost trading and mutual funds.

**quicken.com**  Head to the investment center for info and investment options; you can also download financial and company data.

**troweprice.com**  Investment service and advice from T. Rowe Price.

**financialengines.com**  Noncorporate, private investing advice and portfolio management from Nobel Prize–winning economist William F. Sharpe.

**bankrate.com**  This huge investing and personal finance management site provides "objective" free services, info, advice, and calculators.

**dinkytown.net**  This site should be called "calculator town." Loads of finance and investing calculators, plus retirement planning advice.

**standardandpoors.com**  Look for mutual fund ratings, indexes, and information; company stock info; top-rated investments; stocks in the news.

**moodys.com**  The site of Moody's Investors Service offers mutual fund ratings and information, along with company news, ratings, and research.

CHAPTER

# 10

# A Pricey Future

### *And What Can Be Done About It*

So now you've got some tools to take better control of your money, manage your debts, and hopefully plan your future. Lessens the sting a bit. You should feel very good about what you're doing. But the satisfaction of taking that control certainly doesn't make the ache of tight living go away.

We know how we got here. Does that mean that everyone following in the education line behind you—colleges pumping out debt-laden grads by the thousands—has to go through the same thing, or worse? Given shoddy, top-heavy economic policies, harrowing education costs, and the weak choo-choo of low-ass starting salaries puttering to keep up with the cost of living, will adulthood start at thirty-two in the future, rather than the already delayed twenty-six? Or maybe the next group of young adults will embrace the ways of other less prosperous countries and live permanently with their parents (that means you!)—squished intergenerational homes and limited independence not seen since, oh, I dunno, the Depression? And come retirement time, will we be jilted by Uncle Sam out of the Social Security we've been paying all our working lives—the pool sucked dry by the mammoth-size generation of older adults before us (and the folks they put in Washington)?

Let's do a quick review of what's going on and see what's in the works when it comes to higher education costs, Washington policy, and credit cards and come up with a few ideas on what can be done about it.

## Debt for Diplomas: College Trends and Loan Reform

College tuition fees have gone up faster than any other consumer cost in the past ten years, and that includes outpacing the skyrocketing costs of health care. Earlier, I reviewed the whys and hows of this disturbing tidbit of modern life. However, traditional colleges are starting to hear the horses of competition galloping closer behind, closing in and forcing changes in the current system—at some point.

One growing trend is that cheaper for-profit universities are starting to steal away students. Besides the snob factor, why not? They're run more like the corporations they actually are, and as a result for-profit college fees are much less expensive than the alternative.

In the future, colleges will not only have to compete with new for-profits, but they'll be losing international students and Americans as well to universities overseas. China, Great Britain, New Zealand, Australia, and Germany are all moving full steam ahead, pumping tremendous resources into building high-level English-speaking schools to compete with American ones. And they're succeeding. *The New York Times* recently reported that in 2004, foreign applications to American undergraduate schools fell for the first time in thirty years, and those to graduate schools fell 28 percent. Germany is offering a competitive education for free while Australia and New Zealand are going for revenue, but they're still cheaper than the majority of American colleges. We'd better start reforming or we'll be suffering the kind of brain-drain that Europe and Asia experienced during World War II, when their best and brightest came to the United States not only to escape war, but also to gain access to a wonderful education.

Some colleges are trying to compete by freezing full-term tuition costs at students' freshman-year rate. In the summer of 2004, *The Wall Street Journal* reported that schools that offered to lock in tuition rates for incoming freshmen had higher rates of retention: Students were more likely to graduate within four years and also not to transfer to a potentially less expensive college to finish their education. Some states are also looking to limit annual tuition increases at their public colleges—to a more manageable 4 percent, for example, as opposed to today's trend of 11 percent to 15 percent a year.

Student loan reform has become a bit of a two-headed hydra. On one side you have passage in 2003 of the College Loan Assistance Act, allowing consolidated student loans to carry a weighted APR average not exceeding 6.8 percent. There's also HR 2711, which allows holders of federal student loans to choose a consolidator of their choice—rather than having to stick with the feds for consolidation. Both these workings of Washington help keep the student loan monster a bit at bay by limiting interest rates and offering you choice.

At the same time, however, the Department of Education has become a fierce debt collector. Before 1998, bankrupt graduates were able, for the most part, to be free of their student loans (which they can't pay if they're going bankrupt, obviously) or get them substantially reduced. Well, those days are long gone. Bankruptcy no longer gets you out of paying your student loans, and the government has become vicious about getting its money back. *The Wall Street Journal* ran a front-page story in early 2005 on the ruthlessness of student loan collection. It was reported that if you're delinquent on your student loan now, the Department of Ed will sic a hard-core collection agency on you. It can also garner your wages, Social Security income, and tax refunds without a court order, relieving you of the chance to argue your case. Previously, only the IRS had the power to deny you that right.

Why and how can they do this? Well, they have lots of financial impetus. Student loan default rates are now in the single digits, while about fifteen years ago, one out of five borrowers defaulted. Quite the increase in shakedowns, no? And to think that the government started offering student loans to lessen the burden of college costs.

Another sign that the government is pulling back on helping all young Americans to get a college education—no matter what their household income—is the huge Pell Grant cuts in early 2005. The American Council on Education says that under this new program, the number of Pell Grant recipients will go up, but major city and state newspapers (Detroit, New York, New Jersey) reported that it will also disqualify ninety thousand students currently getting grants, while others will get less aid overall. All this to save the government a seriously measly $300 million. Any thought given to the long-term costs of snuffing out a college degree for thousands of young adults—potential higher-earning taxpayers in the future? This is a time when state legislators (and anyone who stops to think about it for two minutes) know that there is a strong link between the educational attainment of residents and the strength of local economies.

So now that we're becoming an economy that rewards and needs an increasingly educated workforce, how do lawmakers answer? Cut off a hydra head, out sprout two more. Brilliant.

## CREDIT CARD NATION: WILL IT ONLY GET WORSE?

A 2004 Associated Press poll on consumer debt reported that young adults are the group most likely to say that they don't trust themselves with their credit cards. (Probably because they're under the most economic pressure.) The College Board reported a month earlier that up to 25 percent—and counting—of college students use credit cards to help finance their education.

But the biggest report last year on young adults and spending came from Demos, a nonpartisan New York–based public policy group. It reported what we're all too aware of: The young adult population is more likely to be in debt than the rest of the American population as a whole. The report revealed much more, including that slow growth in the take-home pay of twenty-five- to thirty-four-year-olds is not keeping up with inflation. This is combined with a higher unemployment rate in young adults and their student loan debt. The College Board took the average college graduate salary of $36,000 and, after factoring in taxes, housing costs, utilities, food, and transportation, found that only **$34** was left for clothing, child care, entertainment, furnishings, and emergencies. Geesh, last time I checked, money wasn't made of rubber.

Demos puts most of the blame for the stretched and harried state of young adults on credit card companies. The credit card banking industry is **unregulated**! There are no government checks and balances to keep late fees and interest rates and fair business practices reined in. Credit card marketing is a wild machine. Visa offers Visa Buxx, a card designed for parents to give to their kids. Then there are the celebrity credit and debit cards for young teens (Hilary Duff?) and even Hello Kitty cards from MasterCard.

And since there's that amazing $34 left in a young adult pocket to cover basic costs such as clothing and furniture, what about health care? Are credit cards being used because we're a bunch of crazy spending animals? Honestly, sure, there are some of us who buy too many gadgets or shoes. But the majority of young adults are in credit card trouble because they can't stretch their income enough to cover basic necessities—especially with so much money going to pay student loans. Many young adults are uninsured—when and if it's time to go to the hospital, who pays? And what if you're a young parent? Well, if there are two adults at home, you'll both be working to pay for everything, including hundreds of dollars a week in child care. Imagine what a young single parent is up against. (That's for another book . . .)

The answer is, unfortunately, that twelve out of every thousand young adults file for bankruptcy. And it hasn't helped that in recent years there's been a whopping upswing in home equity loans and refinancing of credit cards to lower and lower interest rates—temporary salves. It's merely a juggling of debt from one place to another (yes, maybe you'll have a better rate, but the debt is still there).

## AND THE SOLUTIONS ARE . . . ?

Everyone's got their solutions to the "Generation Debt" problem. Some boomers scold and say that our expectations are too high. We need to get rid of the car and walk two miles in the snow or wait in the scorching sun for a bus, and chuck those cell phones while we're at it. We're spoiled and pampered and want it all right now. Gotta disagree here. Have some young adults lost the will to start out their independent adult lives sleeping in a *cucaracha*-infested apartment on a smelly futon and sharing a broken bathroom with four messy roommates? Sure. But twenty or thirty years ago, that was a rugged choice. Now it may be the only option, and the result of a very expensive yet necessary-to-get-a-white-collar-job education. And those accoutrements of modern life—cell phones, internet access, clean clothes— are now required to get that decent-paying job. The loans for this now necessary education have to be paid from these jobs where the median earnings for young adults (adjusted for inflation) have stayed the same or are less than the late 1970s.

Boomers should be a tad more supportive anyway—especially if they're our parents—because they're the ones dipping into their retirement savings to help us out. Or, as *The Wall Street Journal* recently wrote in "The Coddling Crisis," encouraging our extended adolescence by letting us live at home till we're in our thirties.

In 2004 when John Kerry was running for president, he put forth a plan to give federal college grants to students, who would then, after graduation, spend two years working for the community. He also wanted to extend a tax credit of $4G to parents of college students, and give $10 billion grants to individual states willing to cap their tuition increases at the rate of inflation. He was going to get all this paid for with an overhaul of the government student loan system.

Well, he lost.

Here are some ideas I like for reforming the system that may hopefully, one day, somehow see the light of day:

- Expand access to **health insurance,** especially for part-timers, as well as to other medical benefits and tax-free medical savings plans. If right now you're cut off from your parents' insurance coverage because you're twenty-one or have graduated from college, and it will be another year or two before you can get a job where health insurance is offered or where you'll earn enough to afford your own policy, then the industry needs to extend the time that you can be on your parents' insurance (called **dependent coverage**) to twenty-three, twenty-four, or older. And put pressure on pharmaceutical companies to lower their prices for prescription drugs already!

- Make **student loan deferments** longer (say, a year to eighteen months) so graduates have more time to get on their feet before the student loan bills start coming.

- Push **federal grants** back up to the levels of their inception, when they paid for 70 percent or more of a college education for worthy, needy students. If college costs keep on rising at double and triple the rate of inflation, we're going to end up with an unbalanced set of haves and have-nots—those who can pay for college have, and those who can't have-not. And just because you can pay certainly doesn't mean you're the best and brightest.
- **Regulate the** damn **credit card industry.** Go back to requiring a credit card holder to have a source of income before extending a line of credit. Or, as Demos suggested, require credit card holders under twenty-one to have a co-signer unless they can prove they have an independent income.

  And regulate the practice of hiking up interest rates and slamming cardholders with ridiculous penalty fees for being one day late on a payment. Shameless practices.
- Raise the **minimum wage.** Ten percent or more of young adults with some college education make $8 or less an hour. Minimum wage should at least be linked to the rate of inflation—which, as of now, it has fallen behind.
- Require more **personal finance education** in schools. Right now, sixteen states require some kind of finance education in high school. That's another thirty-four states that need to get up to speed. And in the sad results of a nationwide financial literacy quiz of high schoolers by the JumpStart Coalition for Personal Financial Literacy, the average student answered only 52 percent of the questions right. We are way off in teaching our kids about money management. And this is at a time when kids are spending loads of

money and getting credit cards and debit cards younger and younger. If they're not getting the lessons at home, this basic and very necessary knowledge needs to be taught in school. It's at least as worthwhile and applicable to adult life as calculus.

Young adults are putting off buying a home, getting married, having children, and many other once normal passages of adulthood because they're loaded with debt and can't make ends meet to live on their own. MonsterTRAK.com did a survey in 2004 showing that 57 percent of graduating college students were planning to live back home with their parents after graduation. According to the Census Bureau, in the past twenty years the number of college graduates returning home to their parents went up 14 percent. *USA Today* recently covered this "boomerang-kids" phenomenon and quoted a Harvard analyst who said that he found a **direct correlation** between rising rent prices and the rising number of adult children living with their parents.

Banks have a vested interest in all this, too. Young adults are disproportionately likely to want and need banking products, since they're the most likely to cross certain life markers that require banking products. Let's see, we need student loans, credit cards, first-time mortgages, 401(k)s and other tax-friendly accounts, savings, basic investing, and—when marriage and children come—everything else. This doesn't mean that banks should identify us as a cash cow for their business; rather, if we're not in a position to earn more money, or if we're stuck paying so much to the government for our loans, the banks are missing out on our savings and investing moneys, not to mention selling fewer first-time mortgages. Banks have an opportunity here to step up and help us out with better marketing of their products, better products overall, improved and ethical business practices, and support for financial education.

We also need to step up to the plate and show up at the polls. If only 37 percent of eighteen- to twenty-four-year-olds voted in the 2000 election and a bit more in 2004, the 65-plus percent of us over twenty-five who voted can't pull all the young adult weight. Older generations wield so much power in Washington not just because they're running the show—they put themselves there. They vote, not just at the polls but with their wallets. We can't vote with our wallets as much as they can, but we can pick and choose where and how we get our educations and loans, and we can influence what gets talked about and who's doing the talking come election time. And if we can't fix it for our generation, let's do our best to fix it for our kids. Because guess who'll be paying for college then? You betcha.

## In Parting

I am not just a part of "Generation Debt." I have four younger sisters in their twenties and handfuls of other family and friends who have seen and experienced the struggles of student loans, credit card debt, lack of health insurance, renting, buying a first home, and investing for the first time. I hate to see Generation X and Y struggle so much financially. But I also believe a bit of control and education can make it much, much better.

If you've gotten this book and have read even a part of it, you've taken a big step to getting yourself closer to a financially better place. And no matter how dire your situation, there's nothing to be scared of and nothing to be ashamed of. You'll reap the benefits of what you take care of *now* much sooner than you think.

Best wishes to you. I hope I've helped.

## Web Links

**collegesavings.org**  The site of the College Savings Plans Network is an affiliate of the National Association of State Treasurers. It offers a clearinghouse of information on college savings plans, and monitors changes in federal policies and legislation relating to college savings programs.

**18to35.org**  This nonprofit, nonpartisan policy research site of "America's youth movement" promotes the issues and needs of young adults.

**demos-usa.org**  At the site of research firm Demos, you can view and download the full report on "Generation Broke."

# INDEX